The Flesh of a Whore

and

The Spirit of an Evangelist

Tomitra Odunaiya

2

CONTENT PAGE

God Wants Me To Do This

It is hard for me to talk about it, to talk about this. I really don't want to but I have to because God wants me to.

And that's the problem. God wants me to. I spent years trying to forget that I was a whore, that I am a whore. Now God wants me to talk about it. He wants me to take my darkness and bring it into the light.

But then everybody will know . Everybody will judge me. Then I will get stoned to death.

I know that that seems a little dramatic to say but it is the truth. People words will destroy me. When they open up their mouths to say something about me .Their words will become like rocks and I will get beaten for living a life that I didn't have a choice but to live. It was handed to me and I was force to take it.

Me-God , please don't make me tell.

I look at telling my story like looking in a mirror. I want to move away from the mirror but God won't let me. He makes me look at myself and he says,

God-But you have to.

Me-Nooo.

God-It is time.

Me-I don't want to.

God-You have to.

Me-Can I just move away from my mirror?

God- It is time to let it out . You have no choice. It is eating you up inside.

I wondered what will the world think of me but that is what has kept me quite ,caring about what people will say and think. Will they look at me as the whore or will they see who I really am

God says I have to do this. No matter, how hard it is for me to do, it must be done.

It's not easy to do this, to write about myself and tell my secrets. I know that once I do this , it is out there for the world to see and who is going to want me after they know my secrets. I thought long and hard about my family.

While I was writing this, my friend told me that she would never tell her secrets. She wondered how this would affect my children. What would the world say to them and how would they be treated because of me? Would they be hurt by what I said

I had to wonder, if I was being selfish.

All of this mattered but I kept hearing God say, "I told you not to worry"

You see this was God's idea. It wasn't mine.

I didn't want to do it but I feel as if I had to.

I have to.

The need for me to do this is so much greater.

Now, I didn't know why it was when I began . I just know that if I didn't, nothing would change.

So the book begins .

I Was The Whore

I begin with admitting that I was the whore.

I never wanted to admit it.

I never wanted to say that I was a whore.

That word ,whore…. it makes me laugh because I don't know what else to say. There is no other word to use but whore. People see the smile on my face and they assume that I am happy but I am really crying on the inside. I laugh ,because laughing makes it bearable.

Why bearable ?

I have had to carry that name and accept the fact that , that is who I am.

Bearable, sometimes it is hard to bear it. So yes, I laugh to bear it and to hide the shame of it.

Whore is such a terrible word but it is a word that I have to use. I don't want to use it but it is the word that fits.

You might ask why. Because all of my life, that is what I was forced to feel and to see within myself.

The word whore is the definition of me.

I didn't want to see myself as one, but I can't even see myself as anything else. If I try to tell myself that I am not , well…. I am forced to ask myself,

Didn't you sleep with men ?

And I have to answer, yes. Yes, I did.

I slept with not one, but many men And I had reasons why I did, but no matter why I did it, I did it. When you sleep with a lot of men ,you become a whore.

I wonder, how many men does it take to become a whore? One man can make you a whore., just one

People won't say that is true. Because it is how you look at it. You see, I can say that I am a whore but for years, I refused to believe that I was one. My mentality was how could I be? I wasn't on a street corner selling myself.

The women who did that were the whores. The women on the street corners waiting for a man to stop by and raise his window down. They tell the man what is for sale and how much it cost for them to do whatever the man wants them to do. They put a price on their body. No, that is not me. I wasn't a whore. Or should I say I wasn't one in my mind.

 I could never make myself believe that I was one but my actions were telling me that I must be one.

See, I kept denying it but in my heart, I was feeling like I was one.

 In my younger days, I didn't think about whether I was a whore or not. If you had asked me if I was one at the age of sixteen, I would have told you no. I would have been mad because you asked me. Angry because you thought it.

If you asked me in my twenties , the answer would have been no but I would have wondered if I was one.

Let's say you asked me in my thirties, the answer would have been a no but I would feel like I should have said yes. I would have been too afraid to say it.

Have you been or have you ever been a whore?

Who is going to ask that question? No one

Are you a whore?

I couldn't say yes, even if I wanted to.

Now, I am in my forties and no one has to ask me the question because I ask myself every day and no one hears the answer but me and the answer is yes.

The Beginning

I am not sure when I started claiming that I was a whore. I just started saying it.

I just started believing it and I couldn't deny it any longer.

It's how I felt when I had sex with any man. After I had given him what he wanted; after he exploded in me

He could say that he loved me. He could try to convince me that he cared but he slept with me and that made me a whore.

Did I see him as my john?

No. I don't think that I could allow myself to see that but I did see him as someone who hurt me or took something from me. I know, I know. I gave it to him but it didn't matter because he took it. If he held me afterwards, I would feel safe but they hardly ever held me.. I put my arms around them. I wanted to be close to them and if they wanted me some more. I gave myself to them again.

That's just what you do. They ask by kissing you or touching you and you say yes by letting them inside of you.

I hate to even say that. It makes me want to cry. I am disgusted by it but it is the truth.

When I would hold them, I never saw anything wrong with the fact that they turned their backs on me.

Besides , I was use to sleeping that way. When I was kid ,my sister and I shared the same bed and many nights I would get scared and I would sleep under her to feel safe.

There were moments that I couldn't hold her and it didn't bother me because I knew why and I understood why.

Anyway, what I realize is that you get tired of holding someone and they not hold you.

It is funny because I never knew how important it was to be held. Then I heard this story. A young woman told me that her father died when she was eight and the one memory that she had of him was when she was two years old. She remembered him holding her in his arms and making her feel safe.

I never got that, the safe part.

Many times I was by myself and scared. When I was really frighten, I hid under my bed.

I dare not question myself about why I hid under the bed.

There was a reason. See , if you don't remember ever being held, you may not ever have felt safe.

I can say that I was never safe and that means that I could never feel safe.

I took what I could get . So, no one held me and that meant I had to hold them.

When the men would turn their backs on me that made me a whore because a man don't look at no whore. (doesn't look at a whore) They don't see you while they are on top of you and they don't hold a whore.

That's just the way it is.

I always say that, the way people treat you is how they see you and you continue to let them treat you that way because that is how you see yourself..

I never admitted to anyone that I was a whore, not even to myself. I just felt that I was and I guess that is what tormented me. It was because I knew that I was.
But I didn't want to be one.

Every time that I slept with a man , the goal wasn't to be a whore. It was just the outcome of it.
When I learned to look at myself that way, I hated seeing myself as a whore but for years I remained one.

The Other Woman

I was writing a book called "Knowing Who You Are and I had to do some research on getting to the place that you know who you are. One of the subjects that I wrote about was the alter ego. It was so many positive things about having an alter ego. You could step out of your comfort zone when you portrayed another personality. As I was writing about the alter ego, something came over me and I realized that for most of my life I had an alter ego.

If you asked me if I had one before I wrote about it, I would have told you no and I would have said that I didn't believe in them .But ..I had one.

Most people who have one, give theirs a name. I hear the Lord saying that when you do that you give them more power.

I introduce you to The Whore.

She is every man's dream. She is strong and beautiful. She does what she does and she puts a man to sleep.

She is the whore.

I didn't give her a name because she doesn't deserve one. A whore never gives her real name because it is too personal. I gave her the title that she deserved.

For me, the men knew my name.

I am trying to think, when was the first time some man said my name while they had sex with me.

You know, I hated my real name because of the way my mama said it but wonder if I hated my name because some man said it.. it wouldn't be because he just said it. It would be because of what he was doing to me or I to him when he said it .

I am thinking about it because I loved hearing my name when the men called it. It meant that I was doing something right.

Yes, I made them call my name.

But I wasn't me when they said it.

It hurts me to think about it because when they said my name, I was The Whore.

The whore was in control and strong. She never doubted herself. She felt like something and she was gorgeous . She didn't feel like a mistake.

She thought of no one, not even herself while she was with a man. She only thought of the man.

What about God?

There was no place for God in that moment. You see, The Whore wasn't me.

My only thoughts were of God, when she did not have control. I know that you don't understand and you question it. To be honest, I can't explain it .

It is just what it is.

The Whore had all the power and I had none.

I had to become her to do what I had to do.

I am not a victim in this .I can't admit that. I can't say that I am because I do not feel that it is fair. You see, I loved the way that I felt when she was in control. It was freedom but it was also imprisonment.

Was the whore evil?

I often felt that she was wrong , dirty and even unclean but not evil. She believed in God because I believed in God .

It's just, how do you think about God when a man is on top of you? You are not feeling the Holy Ghost when you are screaming and I know, I know oh so well how we call out God in the act of but we are calling because of a feeling and the feeling is a lustful feeling. Your body is being fulfilled.(if I can say that)   A whore is doing what she doing to survive.

If you don't do it right, you don't get the right feeling. Some whores try to numb their selves, so they cannot feel

Some whores, all they want to do is feel.

I just wanted to feel. It was a high but the high never lasted long enough and it was never greater than the feeling that I got when I felt the Holy Spirit

Loving Her

Did I love the whore?

You could say that I did.

But I never loved her as much as I loved God.

15

Did I love her?

Yes, to some degree, I did.

When I was fifteen ,she became my strength and she stayed that way, as I got older.

I wasn't aware of her or my feelings towards her until now. I just thought that it felt good to give myself to a man. I wasn't the whore when I started. I was me. Then time passed by and I just thought I am a whore(but never wanting to admit me) and I knew that I had to keep it a secret.

When I was a teenager, I loved being her and as I say that, I know that she could never be me.

Why come she can't be me?

She can't be me because why would she be. There was never a desire to be the person that I was.

I say that and then I think to myself that when you have been a whore for such a long time, all you want to do is be somebody different.
But even thinking that doesn't change the fact that I could become her and she could not become me .

Why?

Because as a child, I was the weak one and nobody wants to be the weak one . She was loved .Why would she want to be weak, when we knows that nobody loves the weak one.

It hurts me to say that I loved her and it hurts me to realize that I had to love her.

I loved that part of myself for a very long time. There were moments that if I didn't see her ,I missed her

I missed the power and the control. You wasn't going to notice me but you were going to see her. For that reason alone, I loved her.

I loved her more than I loved myself.. Let's be honest, I never loved myself. I don't want to say it but it's true. I always wanted to die. In some way, she kept me alive.

Was she a reason to live?

I was always one step from death. If it wasn't for her maybe I would have died

But yet I hear God saying that it wasn't her that kept me alive.it was him.

Does that change my feelings for her?

I am just beginning to have the revelation of what the whore meant to me .I am just now hearing God speak to me.

See, I loved her and then I got older and my love for her began to change.

I got to the point that I didn't want to love her.

But , no matter how I felt about her, I still gave her control

Why?

Because I could not see.

How many of us know that we can be blinded by our sins?

As I ask this question, the Holy Spirit says "You didn't make yourself blind. Someone took your sight and you decided to stay blind."

I told myself many times that I wasn't a whore and all I heard was,

How could you not be a whore?

Do you remember how many men you slept with?

You enjoyed it, didn't you?

It was like, I put a spot light on myself.

I could hear myself say, " You are a whore. Admit it. Admit it. Admit it just once to yourself" so, I did. I admitted it ..

Yes, I slept with a lot of men and maybe I enjoyed it

And I kept telling myself , "but and you don't understand".

And I kept telling myself ,"because."

Then I had to say yes, I was a whore.

I don't like saying it and I don't get any joy by saying it but I have to admit it.

God wants me to be me. What is he thinking? I have to be real and tell the truth. Who cares if it hurts or not.

I wanted to make it a story and take the feelings away. I wanted to tell the story and not be a part of it but God wants me to feel every word .

I keep hearing that this will be the greatest thing that I ever wrote because it will set me free.

Okay God. I will do it but it is so hard.

I have to write this and in doing that I have to ask myself the hard questions.

I have to look at myself and judge myself.

This should be easy. I have done that all of my life. I said „it should be easy .

I have to look at myself and be my own interrogator.

Who better for God to use than me.

In my mind I am saying. " me against myself" (the good verses the unclean) .I was watching a show, where the man kept seeing his inner self. His inner self was a monster and I kept thinking how that was me. The man was scared of who he thought he would become. He was scared of the monster because if the monster came out, maybe there would be no going back and that reminded me of the whore.to some degree, I held her captative. I chose to let her out .I was finally being okay and it scares me to think that she could be set free.

I can't do another hundred men. I will just die.

One man is enough for me to kill myself.

I ask myself s God enough for me to live.

At the time that I started writing this, I questioned God because n, I didn't want to but

It's a but

I can't be afraid to ask the hard questions and I must answer them truthfully with no hesitation.

As, I looked at myself I began to think…..

Sex was a part of my life for as long as I could remember I knew about sex at the early age of five or six. I knew that the man had to be on top of the woman and they both had to be naked. I knew that it was done in the darkness and you had to be quite. I knew you never told. I would like to say that I learned it from Her. I will never tell you who Her is but I will say that even though she showed me some things I never saw her as a whore. She wasn't even aware that she showed me these things. No she wasn't the whore, I was.

I questioned myself.

Is that the excuse for how you turned out?

Me-No, it wasn't their fault that I saw them . It wasn't their fault that I laid beside them and knew what they were doing. I touched them and knew that they were naked. I touched them and knew that he was on top of her.

Did you get aroused?

Me-I was just a kid. My mind wasn't there nor my body.

I know someone is trying to guess who Her is but I will never let you know and your guess will not ever be the right answer. I have to say that.

Her is not the issue and telling her secrets won't do me any good because she didn't become the whore, I did.

It would be a crime now, to put her on the stand .God won't find her guilty for the actions that I did

When did you try having sex?

Me-I was six when I would attempt it but I didn't know where things went and either did the boy that I was with. We were just mimicking what we saw. Let's just say that it did not work out. We didn't figure it out that day.

I wanted to see that moment as the beginning but I can't because at six, I still believed I was innocent

Besides, how could that one event open up a door way?

Even I am not sure. I, myself am trying to figure it out and I am trying to understand.

When did it all start? When did I become the whore?

You see being the whore was affecting me. I couldn't just have sex with a man without feeling. I had to feel something before I slept with them. It could have been lust or love .It had to be one or the either. There were times that it was both.

It always started with love or lust but how it ended was the issue. If it was lust, I just had to be present in the moment and stay focus.

In my mind, I am saying "I did my job. I did my job."

When it was love, I gave all of my emotions, Everything was in the action itself. Whichever it was, I did not see it as an issue.

How could it be?

I know the answer. The more you give yourself away the more you hate yourself for doing it.

I was looking for something in the sex and it wasn't there.

Because I lived a life where sex never ended. I began to hate myself more than what I already did. And I hated the men.

Gradually, I came to relizations.in the beginning, I belonged to the man I had sex with. In my mind, it was forever.

Let me not lie to you. There was a time when sex was sex and it was fun and carefree. I did it without a thought. I can't tell you why. I hate myself for those moments but they happened.

All I can say is when I was doing it for love, I belonged to the man and I thought I was okay but as time went by, I knew that I wasn't okay.

The older I got , the more I knew that if any man slept with me ,I would never be his. And I would hate him.

There were moments that I could look at someone and just know. I was pouring out of my body and filling it up with hate and anger.

I use to tell myself that he loved me .I could feel it and see it. He didn't have to do much. Sex use to be enough and then it got to the point that I didn't know if a man loved me or not.

Not knowing was especially hard for me.

Whitney Houston use to sing this song

"How Do You Know If He Loves Me"

Sex was supposed to say that he loved me .I convinced myself of that. Sex was attention and it meant love but I learned that a man can have sex with you all day and not love you. Then sex becomes a weapon against you.

I never thought about it being that way because television doesn't show that. Sex was supposed to make you feel special but when you have had sex as long as I have you

22

look at sex differently. I looked at sex as a weapon against me.

Now I never loved myself and you will hear that again and again but I hated the whore. I hated becoming her and sometimes I had no choice but to be her.

I know you heard me say that I loved her but you also heard me say that my feelings changed for her. My feelings became hate.

See, I had to become her.

Why?

When I was having sex with these men, it was because I cared for them, I became her.
She couldn't get hurt. No, not while she was in the moment but me,…when she was done, I was the one hurting.

Always me.
I got the…" I don't want you"

I got the.. "I will sleep with you and then I will leave you"
Was it always that way?
No but there were moments that I didn't know the difference.

Was I Free

God made me see myself through the years. You can't imagine how many times I erased the word myself in that one sentence. I wanted to put the whore but I couldn't type it. I kept seeing the word "myself."

It was so much easier to see her and not me. I know we are one but I promise you, we are separate. She only knew man and I knew God.

Why was God making me do this? I really didn't ask that question. I guess, I kinda knew that God was making me look back through the years at her , at myself to get to me.

It's like I was always being reminded of her. I started out sleeping with one guy, then another and another. I lied and I cheated and each time I was filthy. I was a dirty rag in my mind, and I could not be cleaned.

It was after I moved by myself that I decided that I wouldn't be the whore any more.

During that time ,I wasn't sleeping with a lot of men. I passed the years of man after man.

So at any time ,I could say I am not the whore but I knew it did not matter whether I slept with one man or a million., I was the whore.

The only way not to be one was to stop having sex.

I was a good girl who only slipped up every now and again.

Don't think that I didn't get punished for it because I did.

By who? By God/

No but by me. The guilt of letting God down and the betrayal . I betrayed God and myself every time I slept with a man.

I would like to say that they went against God when they slept with me , but can I even say that?

Let's leave it at, they hurt me.

Anyway, time went by and I hadn't slept with a guy for a minute(some time). I finally felt okay. I mean, I didn't think about the whore anymore.

I won't say that there weren't any urges but nothing became of them.

Did I feel free?

I felt okay. I don't think I looked at it as freedom.
She was freedom.

Then I met this guy and we talked. I remember talking to him about God and you know that excited me. I felt a connection. I felt like a good girl. I also remember the moment he and I talked about sex.

I told myself that it was all in fun

Did you think you were being a whore then?

No because to me the whore was not manifested in words. Yes, it got me in the mood but again nothing happened. The whore emerged through sex . The whore was sex.

There were some things that he said that made me think but when you don't want to see something, you don't see it.

At that time I wanted love and I wanted to believe that this guy was love.

You know how they say faith of a mustard seed, think of love that way. That's all I needed to make love to a man.

It's not even love anymore for me. It is just sex. I made love to people who didn't love me.

I say that, because I and this guy did everything but have sex. He saw me naked. I made myself believe that it was okay. It was okay, even though he told me that we were friends. What was wrong with seeing me naked .Nothing was going to happen but I have to ask myself are those whorish ways?

I remember making the decision to just have sex with him. Why would you do that?

To see how he felt.

I didn't ask for a promise

Everything was based on. "until he said otherwise". I was hoping for him to say otherwise

But you know after I did it, I thought something would change.

Nothing changed except, I kept having sex with him .I kept having fun with him.

You asked if I felt free and I said freedom was not on my mind at the time but as I think about this moment, I realize that the whore was tied up and slowly, I was setting her free.

I can't say that she made any decisions because I know her. I feel like I opened the door.

When I realized that she was free, (that part of me) I didn't like it. I didn't want to give her total freedom. See, she was free but she could only go so far. I was determined not to grow old as the whore. So I told this guy who I loved that I had laid on my back for years and that I did not want to do it anymore. We were having sex together for almost a year. I had never been with someone that long who did not make me his woman.. After a year, he had not said he loved me or that we were in a relationship. It bugged me. I had spent a lifetime being tormented by sex or the men that had sex with me. I spent years trying to escape that life and here this person comes bringing this life style back. I should say bringing her back. Who is her? She is the whore and I hate her. I HATE HER! You see, the whore is me and I hate myself. When I told him that I couldn't be her anymore, he was upset. He said he cared about me but his actions were something different.

In that moment he became a hindrance to who I was trying to be but I couldn't just blame him. He didn't understand my life and he didn't know how much power the whore really had. She had already revealed herself to him and he didn't even know. I thought should I blame him for being a man? Should I hate him for being a man but how could I? As he pointed out, I did my part. I had kissed him and I touched him. Sometimes, I started it. In my defense , I didn't want it to lead to sex.. I wanted us to play around like teenagers and do nothing. I wanted innocence.

I remember telling him "You just don't get it".

I needed to know that with him I was safe and if I didn't feel safe there was problem.

He would come over to my house and have sex with me and then in the morning leave me without a word of who were we to each other and every time he did that I felt like a whore.

Why continue to do it?

I hate that question because I don't have an answer. Maybe because that's all I knew. Maybe because I loved him. Maybe I just knew I was the whore

No, I won't accept that I knew I was the whore. I didn't want to be her. I wanted love.

Did you know that" want" is a tool that Satan uses. When you are desperate for that want, you will wait, accept and do anything for that want.

So ,I blame myself and I can't help but to blame the guy. He said that he knew God and after a year, he knew me. He knew that I wanted more than a man between my legs.

You know that I can't help but to see Satan in this moment.

Why say that?

Because it is like Satan was using him to get to me. Oh yes, Satan was a part of this. I spent years trying to get away from him and Satan always found me . I finally got away from him and I was determined never to go back. So, Satan used this person to try and take me back to a place that I already been.

After all that I had been through to finally be free and for Satan to try and take me back.

I questioned myself. Was I free?
I slept with this man without a commitment accepting it for what it was. That does not sound like I was free.
Maybe Satan just extended the chains.

Friends

I stood in the hallway of my job and I prayed to God for a friend .

Why?

Because I did not know how to be a friend to a man. The men I knew were acquaintances. I would see them at work but not hang out with them and the men that I hung out with became my lovers. I did not know what real friendship was.

That was pointed out to me by a guy I slept with. He didn't say those words. He just said that we were never friends. Because he said that, I wanted a man in my life that I could be a friend to and love.

As soon as I prayed, he showed up. I thought that he saw something in me.

Now I wonder ,if the something was the whore.

When I was with this person, I didn't feel like a whore. I didn't feel loved either. It is sad because every time I watched him leave , I ached with guilt and I didn't know why. I was trying to avoid what I was feeling. I realize that watching him close the door affected me. It wasn't always like that .We use to hug each other, but I think that after being with him(having sex) and just being "a friend". What is that "a friend" You can sleep with me and accept my body but not want anything else. I excepted his terms for who we were and what we were going to be. I was hiding my feelings. I was giving the whore life. You would have to understand that the whore was created a long time ago and she was a part of my life, ever since I can remember. Let's just say The whore was a part of my life for a long time. I finally got rid of her and it wasn't easy. Then he comes a long and it starts all over again.

I have to ask myself, will she ever leave and be completely gone. If she came back once and twice, why wouldn't she always come back.

I remember before he came, I thought she was gone. I was never sure of it but I wanted to believe it.

There was a time that I would say ,I am so scared that she will come back and I would have to ask myself was she really gone, knowing that she could come back and destroy me.

How Was The Whore Conceived

The older I got , the more I wanted her to leave but she would not go away, not completely.

I thought, but why? Where did she come from. How did she get here.
The more I questioned myself ,"how was she conceived?"
I knew my birthday. I knew my mama and my daddy and I had a name but her.
I knew that she was formed and I figured she began when I first had sex the first time. I didn't know it for sure. It was just a guess. It was only a guess.
Now in the beginning, I wasn't worried about how the whore was formed. I didn't know she existed and when I suspected that she was there, I didn't think that she was growing with me. It didn't matter when she was formed. What mattered was that she was there. Then, why does it bother me that I don't know when she took her first breath?

See, I knew the whore was affecting me but I thought wishing her away was enough.

Let me be honest, I was praying her away and it wasn't working.. You will hear that a lot. It wasn't working. I think that I got to the point that I asked myself when was the whore born. I didn't need a year or a certain day. I needed a reason and a moment . I wanted to know what happened to me that made her be formed. I asked the question but I didn't want the answer.

See, I think I kind of knew but I didn't want to relive the moment she was conceived.

So, I tried to block the question out of my mind. I knew if I blocked the question ,I wouldn't remember what happened.

I guess that I could say that I had to do it that way because I was afraid to admit the moment she cried out

But that the thing, she didn't cry out in lust.

I keep seeing the moment that the woman is on top of the man and her tilting back her heard crying out in gratification because that's what I thought all these years. The whore started out with love. I could be alright if that was the case. I didn't want to see any other moment. I could wrap my head around the fact that I was addicted to love and that made the whore. Any other way would destroy me.
It's funny because I was trying to remember it that way and not to remember the real moment and God, he wanted me to remember the truth.

God says "Remember"

 And I say "There is so much that I have forgotten about my life"

31

I told God that I was okay with that but God wasn't.

and I was okay with not knowing but I guess God wasn't.

See, to answer the question of when the whore was born, I had to remember.

"Wait," I begged God.

Because I honestly didn't want to remember.

I can't say that it was God or not but my mind kept wanting to answer the question.

I was so afraid but God said, "The question was asked and now the truth has to come out."

Touches

When I was very young, older boys from my mother's church would find me in darkness and touch me. I let them touch me . I am not sure if I liked it or not. I don't know how I felt about it. It was something that they did. I do not know if I saw it wrong or not .I just knew not tell.

Some people will say that I had to know it was wrong and they will judge me for it. They will say that I liked it and didn't care if it was wrong. But like I said, all I knew was not to tell.

I was so young at the time. I was felt so alone as a young child. So when the older boys came to me and touched me , I don't know....I didn't think about wrong or right.

Maybe, I felt special. I didn't think about liking it. Maybe it was the attention.

I know, I had God. I knew God but I wasn't aware of him. I didn't know to call out for him. The touches were a game to me.

I often thought that God made me and I was a mistake. I can't say whether I was mad at god because I know I loved him . I just couldn't believe that I was anything more than a mistake. Especially when you have people showing you that you are a mistake. These boys they wanted me.

Again I questioned myself.

The interrogator- So you wasn't threatened to be quite.

Me-These older boys knew me. They knew that I wouldn't say anything.

The interrogator- Did you think no one would believe you?

Me-I don't know.

The interrogator And when they were done, how did you feel?

Me-I can't remember. I don't remember feeling special and I don't remember being afraid when they did it again.

Come to think about it, that is the reason that they were able to touch me.

The interrogator Why?

Me-Because I didn't feel special.

The interrogator- So ,you want people to feel sorry for you, when you let this happen

Me-I do and there are times that I do not want to tell anybody because of the guilt that I have for letting it happen.

The interrogator- Will you say that you were molested?

Me-No.

The interrogator -Why?

Me-Because I didn't say no . Because I didn't try to say no.

The interrogator But you were just a kid.

Me-So, who cares. I had a voice And I didn't use it.

The interrogator- Did it ever cross your mind that Satan didn't want you have a voice.

Me-What are you saying? It never crossed my mind. I just thought that Satan wanted my body.

The interrogator And he got it?

Me-Yes, he did.

The interrogator- So you gave your body to him?

Me-No, I didn't .

The interrogator But you said that you let those boys touch you.

Me-I know But I had no choice. In my mind, I had no choice.

The interrogator- And did you hate the men?

34

Me-No, not when I was a child. How could I hate them for something that I did, that I let them do.

The interrogator Did you ever hate them?

Me-When I got older and became aware of what they did.

The interrogator What do you mean?

Me-I always thought that they did nothing wrong .I said yes. So because of that ,I never saw it as a bad thing. If anyone ever asked who has been touched in this place, I never raised my hands. But there was a time that I had to deal with it and realize..

The interrogator Realize what?

That the guys who touched me were wrong and I was sicken by it. I never felt nasty until I became aware.

Aware

I think that I remember being touched in my twenties but I chose not to talk about it. I explained why. Some people will say that maybe my mind could not process it. I don't see it that way. Maybe it was a horrific thing but no. all I know is for a very long time I forgot about it .

Then, I met this great guy. We talked on the phone daily and I was starting to have feelings for him. It was time for us to get together. I wanted him to come over to my house. I remember being so lonely and he came into my life and I was so excited. When I opened the door and saw him, all these feelings rushed in. He was sitting on the couch when I kissed him. That should have been it, but I couldn't stop kissing him. I hated myself for what happened next.it all got out of hand.

He began to start touching me. At first I liked it. The touches felt so good. I felt as if I needed them. His hands were so strong .but then…

This is the part that I do not want to talk about.

God, please don't make me talk about it.

I almost have to whisper it . it feels like a secret. You know the rule for a secret, don't you?

You don't tell.

I am scared to tell it and I don't know because he would never hurt me.

I don't want to tell, it's a secret.

I have to ask myself is that the excuse that I am going to use. That is just an excuse not to face it.

Knowing if someone was saying that I would be saying

"How can you say that? An excuse? You are not me!"

And that will make them be quite but since I am asking myself the question , I have to answer it.

He touched me in a place that many men have touched me but not like he did. It took back to when I was a child and before I knew it I was rolled up in a corner. I made him leave.

He had to. There was no way he could stay.

He had to leave touch that touch made me hate him.

Right now, someone is asking why. It reminded me of something that I had forgotten.

It reminded that someone touched me there when I was a child .

Many times I heard about molestation but I never let my mind go too far. When he touched me

it made me see that I was molested and I didn't want to see that. It made me feel dirty.

I didn't blame him for the way I felt .I just hated him for making me remember.

He took me to a place that was ugly; a place that I had forgotten. He made me see what it really was.

I could never say the word molested and that day I was forced to say it. I stopped being the forty something year old woman to the seven year old. Why did they touch me? I never ask for them to.

That is not the question that I want to ask. I know myself well enough to know that what I wanted to know was why did I allow it.

I knew the answer. I didn't know how to say no.

And just saying that to myself was too much because then I wondered is that what made me the whore.

I didn't want to answer that either. I couldn't tell myself if they made me a whore or not.

I went back and forth with it .constantly telling myself "I don't want to say"

Why come I don't want to say? Maybe because I think it made you one?

I know that it was the beginning of me becoming one. I didn't realize it at the time but that's what it was.

That one small event made me into what I am right now?

It doesn't seem so small. It was a big event in my life. It defined me and it created an alter ego. I had to lose myself to become her.

The Name

Who is HER?
She is the whore.
That's what I call myself.
It is funny because I never gave her a name. I gave her a title based upon our action. She is the whore.
I laughed when I think about it.
A name .No, she didn't need a name. When men are on top of you , they do not care about a name.
She didn't deserve a name. Whores, they don't get names. People only know them for selling their selves.
If I had given her a name , I don't think that I could have been set free. Your creator, your mother or father gives you a name and the whore she didn't have a family. So she didn't need a name.
Even in the Bible, the woman at the well was remembered for being a whore. She didn't have a name.

Jesus Saved Her

I had to remember that the whore in the Bible was remembered because Jesus saved her. He gave her a new life.

He protected her?

But she was a whore and why come he didn't protect me?

Interrogator- Are you bitter towards God.

Me-I use to be.

Interrogator-So, you are mad at God?

Me- Am I mad at him? I was mad at him and I loved him all at the same time. I have issues with the fact that he should have saved me.

Did he decide not to. I don't want to ask the questions like was I a bad girl. I was only a mistake. Maybe to friendly. Did I deserve/ Now that is the question to ask.

But I am saying to myself that if he protected the woman in the Bible, then surely he must have protected me.

Maybe I didn't know how he protected me but he did. I have to believe that he did.

I often call out to him asking why. Why me?

Why did it happen? I know I let it happen. Again, it was my fault.

I know but why did they want me? Why did they come into my room?

I never understood why I would hide under my bed at night. I always thought it was because of dad. They always told horror stories about him but wonder if it was something more. I remember not wanting no one to find me or get to me. I knew a grown person could not fit under the bed.

It was scary at night. I always felt that something was after me. Could it be because the boys always came to me in darkness and I couldn't deal with it while it was happening but late at night my safety was under my sister and during the evening time up under my bed . I was safe there.

Again I take the blame for being in a place that they could get to me. So many times I was in darkness.

That is where I would go to be alone.

Actually it was my room that I would go to. I would sit in my room with the lights cut off .

I wonder did I give them a signal to come into the room. I never asked them to come or expected them to come. I went in my room to hide and I usually was alone.

I didn't want to be. That is just the way it was. I never fitted in. I could be in a crowded room and still be alone in a corner.

Interrogator-Did you choose the corner?

Me-I never chose the corner.

No, I was forced there.

No one included me, so I stayed out of peoples way. I did my own thing alone. My corner became darkness.

And that made it easy for the men to come to me. No one was watching over me or looking for me. As far as they knew, I was okay.

But God was supposed to be. I struggle with whether he was there or not. I struggle with whether he was protecting me or not

I know we are not talking about God. We are talking about men. But what about God?

He let it happen and then he turned his back , so he could not see them touching me.

Interrogator- Do you believe he was wrong? Do I feel some type away?

Me-I have to ask myself was it God's will?

No matter what the answer is, I still love God. The Bible doesn't say that we will not go through something.

Can I blame God after all this time? No because I didn't know it when I was a child, but I know it now. I know it was satan.

And my belief gets tested because God sees and knows everything. So, did he allow Satan to reach me in such way I was just a kid.

And I hear something or someone say "He never turned his back on you. He watched over you and made sure that all they did was touch you."

If he let them touch me, then again why? That's all I want to know. Should I blame him? Do I blame him?

And do you blame him?

Yes, I do. He has all power. He could have stopped them.

But how do I know that he didn't?

They could have done worse to me, but they didn't. They did enough. They damaged me.

So, do I accept that and blame God? Again, I know it was Satan. Can I blame God for something Satan did?

God gives us free will. We make decisions and Satan is the one who controls. When it comes to him we don't have anything free. Satan takes things by force. He kills and destroys.

If I saw it that way, I would have to believe that God lets him do it. And what reason does God has to hurt me?

I try to understand it but I question my own thinking. God gave us a mind to decides so did I decide to let them touch me?

That is too much to process because I couldn't decide . In my defense , I was a kid and couldn't make my own decisions.

I tell myself, God knows that you didn't have a choice. Somethings just have to happen. God knows that the men could have chosen to do the right thing. They could have chosen him.

You know I don't remember the touches lasting for years. The young boys had to move.

And so it makes me believe that it was God who moved them.

Some of them were preachers sons. They knew God. I find that just because you know God doesn't mean you choose him and just because your mother or father chooses God doesn't mean you automatically do. Just because someone knows God doesn't keep them from committing acts of crime.

They got to live a life with no issues. They got to be successful and not crazy. They picked me because they knew I would not tell .not just that but I would never tell. Even now I protect them.

They were evil and they knew that they were monsters. I didn't hear them calling out to God. Hopefully they were filled with guilt and changed from their evil ways.

Some people might say that they were not in the wrong. Maybe I am lying because I never told on them. Maybe the boys did nothing wrong .

People will take up for them but I know what happen. I was destroyed in some way by their touches.

And I will never know why. I wish that I could ask them why.

Did someone touch them and if that is the case why did they not tell?

Am I taking up for them?

No, I just want to know why?

But you see, I know that they didn't get off scot-free. If I know my God, I know that he dealt with them.

As a child I didn't know to cry because you were touched. I just knew to take it but now that I am older , I know I can cry for the little girl who was damaged.

They stole a piece of my innocence. That's why I know it was Satan because he steals whatever he can take from you.

He couldn't take my love for God. He couldn't take my soul. So he took my innocence.

All this time I didn't think that I needed to forgive them but the Holy Spirit says that I need to give them that. I don't see a need to forgive. I want to give them nothing. People say that you forgive so that you can move forward.

Me-God if I forgive them will I have peace?

God-Peace is always with in me

Me-Look what they did?

God-You are not that little girl anymore.

Me- I am giving them nothing. They destroyed me.

God-You are not destroyed.

Me-If I am not then I feel like I am .

God-But it is just a feeling that you can let go of at any time.

Me-It owns me. How can I let go of it?

Now that I am aware of it, the touch. It is like ghost; it haunts me.

I know that I must make peace with it all.

Peace with it.

Peace with God.

The Very First Time

I had sex for the first time, when I was twelve. It was with a guy that I loved very much.

I would like to believe that I knew love at eleven. Even with everything that I had been through, I knew love not hate. I looked at him and fell in love. He was there when I needed someone Many people have said to me that at eleven, I was too young to fall in love ,but I disagree.

God says that love is everything . As I look back over this life, I realized if it wasn't for this boy ,I would not have made it. My life was meaningless until he came.
I liked other boys but I loved him. Because I loved him, we made love, a year later

Once when I told this story, a woman asked me was he included with the molesters. You might ask why? I think they asked because he was three years older than me and he had sex with me. The answer is..

I never saw him as a molester. How could I? Besides, I didn't see being touched as being molested. Why would I see making love as being molested? Should I have thought that he molested me ? No. I knew the difference I the touches, I couldn't describe it but I knew the feeling.

The men who touched me , did not have sex with me and I didn't see being touched as making love. So, what was I going to compare to making love to? The men who touched me meant nothing. By that time, I had blocked it out. I loved my first love so much. He was it to me , but I didn't love him more than God and my love for him was different than my love for my uncle .I didn't just accept his touch. I was present in it. I wasn't just doing it. He was my world.

I was so happy with him. He made me feel special.

I remember when he made love to me. It was wonderful I knew it was wrong but I loved him. So, I prayed to God before I did it. I asked God to forgive me.

I wanted God to understand why I was making love to this guy. It was because of love. I convinced myself, no I hoped that God had forgiven me . You see, no matter what happened, I wanted to be loved by this boy who made everything okay for me.

No matter what happened ,I could say at least I prayed. Sometimes I ask myself ,why did I even pray. I knew it was a sin and I knew that I should ask for forgiveness But I don't know, what compelled me to do it before I committed the sin. I just had to. And once I had sex with him, I embodied love. So, I associated love with making love and making love was wonderful. I just didn't know that by having sex with him would make me want to have sex with anyone to have that feeling.

Mama Always Said

My mama always called me fast which is term for liking too many boys. I only liked one but I guess you could see me as fast.

Someone asked, did I fault my mother for what happened to me. In anyway was she the blame?

When I was a child, the answer would have been a no. I didn't even know what I was becoming to blame her. But as I got older, yes. I blamed her because she spoke it. She said I was fast.

Maybe she could see some things about me where she knew that I would be a whore.

I wonder, if she could see those things. If I fixed my mind to believe that she knew ahead of time of who I would be , then I would have to ask a question. Why come she didn't speak the opposite?

By telling me every day about how fast that I was willed it to happen.

It manifested by the words that came out of her mouth

She told me who I was going to be and she had no regrets. Maybe she had them but I never saw the regret.

The Holy spirit asked if I ever heard her say I told you so.

And the answer is no. She never said that but she never said that she was proud of me . Not once did she hold me or tell me that she loved me. I don't know if that would have been enough to stop the things that happened to me. It's not about what happened to me. I wonder what it had been enough for me to stop doing what I was doing.

I always felt that I wasn't good enough. I could never be her.

The Teacher

I learned that men have expectations for you. They act like
you should know how to already do things and if you
don't, they will teach you. There was this guy who asked me
to do more than just lay down with him. He wanted me on
my knees. Did he become God? No . I want to say no but I
am not sure. My mama taught me to never get on my knees
for any man . This guy asked me to. You can only imagine
why.. I had never done it before. And what he wanted I
didn't know how to do. Let me just say that he got mad and
he slapped me.
Even thinking about it makes me rub my face .
I would like to say that I was mad at him but no , I was just
shocked. I might have thought that I didn't like getting hit. I
left after he hit. See, I hurt him
I think I felt that I had to learn to do some things in order to
be good at it and not get hurt. It made me upset if I didn't
know how to do things right.
This guy didn't know it but he was teaching me.
When I think about stuff like that .I feel my mistakes. If I
could go back and tell myself that you should never go down
on your knees for a man. The whore would say if you go
down on your knees be prepared to do what needs to be
done. It is too late to change your mind.
I tell myself that we can't look upon man as a god. If you are
on your knees for a man, what is it costing you. Does it cost
you your dignity?
When man teachers you his ways and his ways are evil, you
give him glory and honor and he becomes a god.
Were these men a god to me? No , they were my addiction
but is that not a god. I didn't see it that way. They were not
the God.

My Sister Is Not A Whore

I wish that I could have been my sister

My sister, she never had to go through what I went through. She had a good life. No one ever touched her or was going to touch her. My sister had a strong mind and she knew who she was. She was going to tell if someone touched her. I wish that I had been her .I wished that I could have fought back. But I didn't know how. To be honest, I never thought about fighting back.

Do I blame my sister for being stronger than me?

No. I look at my sister as a strong woman. I can't blame her for the sins of the men who touched me and had sex with me. It wasn't her fault. Do I wish that it had of been her? I never thought about it. I can say that I knew it wasn't going her and it couldn't be her. When it came to being touched, I didn't have the feelings of being mistreated or hurt. I wasn't angry about it I didn't know to be mad.

Making This About Family

The funny thing is, I have gotten passed this already.

I thought I did. I have dealt with this but that is the problem. I only dealt with it so far. It's like being at a swimming pool and only putting your feet in. You know you need to go deeper but the fear of drowning keeps you from swimming into the deep..

Am I mad? I am not mad.

49

I don't even know why I have to write this and tell this part of my life.

I get chills when I have to admit to something.

You see, what I am dealing with is the whore.

It is so easy to make this about my family because that is what I have done all of my life.

I guess it is because they were not there to stop the things that I had been through but I can't blame them.

Yes, I felt some type of way about my mother but not because of the men I slept with . I always felt that I was treated different.

My sister, she was the best and she was going to make it no matter what. She actually did. But me all I could be was the whore. Anything else was wishful thinking.

I didn't choose an education, a better life. I chose men.

And I still don't know why.

My mama cried for me and when I would run away, she would look for me .

I never saw it as a big thing. I just thought that she didn't want me to be happy.

I never thought that through her, God was trying to protect me from what was going to happen to me.

What about my father?

My father could not protect me. He was lost. He was in a darkness of his own.

50

I wish that I could say that I didn't tell him because he was going through some things but again I didn't see that anything was wrong. I thought it was okay to be touched .I was used to it .

It would be so easy to blame my whole family. Actually, I already did that but I know that it is not their fault.

Should I blame myself?

God Knew

Me-God, you knew what was going to happen to me? Again, why didn't you stop it?

I want to say that it was too late for him to stop it but we are talking about God. It's never too late

I hear the Holy Spirit

Holy Spirit-You had to be willing.

Me-Willing

I don't' understand it because when you need help , you get help.

I question God for being the whore. You see, Jesus didn't come to me and ask me to drink from the water. I wonder if he had, would I have said yes. I was so young. I wasn't tired of the life yet. I convinced myself to live the way I was living.

Maybe I had to be willing to accept help. I had to be willing to ask for help.

I was telling this story to my friend, Jackie and I told her that when I was young, I went to a psychiatrist..

She asked me ,why did I go to one

And I told her that it was because I was acting out.

She asked me why was I acting out.

I had no answer for her. I couldn't pinpoint the reason.

Then she asked if I ever thought that I was acting out because I had been touched.

No, I told her. I mean , why would being touch cause me to act out. Actually, I didn't think anything was wrong with me.

Back then, I blamed my family for how they were treating me .

So, when I tell the story of going to the psychiatrist, I just mention the fact that I didn't like the doctor.

Now I have to wonder, why I didn't like him

I wonder, did I not like him because maybe I knew that he could find out my secret. Subconsciously did I feel that he could figure it out?

If that is the case , then I know Satan would not have allowed that.

Why?

Because, if it was to come out ,Satan couldn't use me anymore. Healing would have begun.

I realized back then, that . Satan could use me for sin and destroy me at the same time.

52

He stole moments from me and killed my innocence and tried to destroy my very existence He wanted me dead..

I always tell people that the psychiatrist wanted to lump me in a percentage and I thought that was stupid because I did not fit into any percentage.

I never went back to that doctor and now I wonder why.

I thought I had something to do with that but now I don't know.

Maybe I was so good at covering up that secret that he felt I didn't need help or maybe my mom couldn't afford it .

Did I still act out?

Yes and I never thought being touch was the reason. See back then , I was mad and defensive .I made it about my family because I didn't see being touched as a problem.

Everything Was About Sex

Everything was based on what I was going to do. I chose love but my love was just an illusion.

The first person I made love to hurt me.

He left me. I cried broken hearted.

So he took something from me and left me with nothing.

I gave it to him willing.

This is the same thing that I said about the men who touched me.

I was willing.

When my first love left me, I was so upset. How was I going to survive?

I don't think that I saw it as survival. I missed him but it wasn't about him. I see now that I needed to be with someone to feel and that was survival.

I needed love to survive.

Love. It sounds funny now. What I mean to say is attention.

Why?

Because that's what I knew.

I fixed my mind to believe it was love.

Given Away

I was given to his best friend.

As I think about it, given… I am trying to see myself as a slave. In reality I wasn't but maybe I was.

The guy I loved persuaded me to like his friend. So, I went with his friend. We didn't make love.

No, he did worse. He just touched me with his finger . I dare not say where and he kissed me.

I know I say he because there is some anger but it is only a little anger. I cannot be mad.

I was a willing partner. I can't be upset at him. I am ashamed of myself because I didn't care enough about myself.

I liked him because he was kind but I never loved him.

I felt sorry for him. He was a decent person. That is what I told myself.

We went on a group outing with our church. We went to the fair and he won me all of these gifts. I can't deny it . I was happy . So, I called that happiness love. I kissed him without thinking and I let him touch me .

I never said stop!

No, I didn't say stop and that's why I ashamed because I let it happen.

Did I let him touch me because I owed it to him.?

He did spend his money on me.

Should I call myself a whore for that?

Or did I let him touch me because I liked him and I liked the attention?

Should I call myself a whore for thar that?

You see some of this is not their fault. Do I blame them and myself for being young? Do I accept the staring roll of The Whore?

Prisoner

Holy Spirit-Can I ask you, what did God give you?

Me-What ? He gave me nothing.

Holy spirit-What about Jesus?

Me-Yes God gave his son to save the world but I wasn't even born yet.

Holy Spirit-But you were included. Why did you give yourself willing to men and not to God?

Me-I gave myself to God. I gave him my soul.

Holy spirit-Did you give him everything?

Me-Don't you get it. Satan had already had me. He kidnapped me when I was so young. He held me prisoner using my body. I didn't know that he had me 'till much later

Most people look at addictions as just addictions .Why would you look at them any other way but in the spiritual realm these addictions are chains and strong holds. Satan has you then. When something bad happens in our lives we say it's Satan but do we know the depth of it. Satan will confuse you and make you think that it is all in fun or whatever and you never really know that it is Satan. I don't know how many men that I slept with before I knew that this was just me sleeping with a man. Satan had me.

At some point in my life, I knew. I would be lying if I told you that I did not want to die but surviving was more important than dying. I didn't even think of it as surviving. I was just living the best way I could.

Learning

I gave the men what they wanted . I willed my period to stop so that I could please them. I learned them. You have to learn them. You have to learn where you can touch them . I learned to ignore their bad breath. I learned to ignore the way they smelled. I learned them so I could give them the best of me. All the while, I fixed my mind and said it was love

But

It only lasted for moments at a time. I made them feel good and I felt good.

There were times that I didn't feel so great but they would never know it. I learned a high tolerance of pain. So if it hurt while they entered me ,I didn't say nothing .I endured it. I learned to take on their weight. They could fall sleep on me and I could still breathe. I realize now that I was taught to take on their weight before this even happened. The times that someone pushed on my stomach or hit me in the stomach. I learned to take it and not get the wind knocked out of me .

There were times that I smiled because I was proud of myself for doing it..

I just keep thinking that I did my job, that I pleased them.

Yes, I taught myself. I didn't have a pimp to keep me in line. Why would I? There was no reason . I didn't have other whores to teach me. Everything I learned , I learned on my own

I learned to see right through them if I was looking at them. I was never trying to see them. Most of the time, I was concentrating on serving them. I had to give them what they wanted. It was all about them. I would close my eyes so that I wouldn't be distracted.

It wasn't always like that. It just depended on who I was with and what I was having sex for.

When It Was Over

And after it was over

Well, that's when reality hit me.

What do you mean?

I was another person when they were on top of me. I wasn't me. I was her. I was the whore. I was good at my job.

But

I had to fix my mind and every part to say it was okay. See, when I said it was love , it made it okay to sleep with them. I could go there and be there in the moment . I was fine with it.

Then..

It would be over and I would see who I was and cry for what I had did.

I cried because they didn't want me. I was just around for sex.

When it was over, I couldn't be the whore. It offended me when they still treated me like one. When they got up from on top of me and acted like I didn't exist, it made me upset; because I thought love was supposed to come after sex.

Did You Kiss Them

The number one rule is not to kiss them in the lips. Kissing makes it personable. So the ones that I didn't love, I did not kiss on the lips and the ones I loved I kissed them. Sometimes they wouldn't take me moving my head as a no I don't want to kiss you, so I had to kiss them. I kissed their alcoholic breaths. I learned to taste myself on their months

Yes. They would kiss my body .They would kiss my sweat. Then they would put their tongue in my mouth and I would taste myself. I didn't even care about what I was tasting . Some of them didn't have the decency to brush their teeth . I had to taste nastiness and not let it bother me. I knew where on their face to kiss them and how to kiss them. As I grew up so did the kissing.

I use to smile about what I had taught myself. Now I just get sick and I thank God that I am in my right mind because I would die if I wasn't.

Smile And Be Sweet.

No matter smile and be sweet.

Men love the sweet, innocent girl.

When I was younger, I use to say that I would never grow up. I always thought that I got this from Peter Pan . I never thought for one moment that it had something to do with the whore but I can't escape the thought that it did. You see most man want the young vibrant girl. They don't want the woman. They want someone to say daddy or a naive girl. They want you to be playful and say yes. They want you to be sweet and give them what they need. They don't want any complaining. You have to stay sweet.

I knew that I would have to stay a little girl. There were moments when I was my age but most of the time I kept the young girl mentality. I never played a game to be that way. It was just what I did. I didn't want to grow up. In my twenties, I was still acting like fifteen. It worked for me. I never lied about my age . I just portrayed someone younger.

I question myself

Did I need love from a man because my daddy was not around?

They say people like me gravitate to men because we don't have a daddy to love us.

I hear God saying "But I was your daddy"

I am trying to figure it out in my mind. You see, the men treated me like I was a cute little girl

And I smile when I think about that part

But then I close my eyes in terror because I know I was woman in their beds. No matter how old I was, they kissed me like I was a woman and touched me like one.

When we got into their beds or wherever ,I had to grow up.

I had a job to do.

I don't want to talk about this anymore.it makes me sick.

Staying Innocent

I realize now that in my mind I wanted to be the child because I lost my innocence. When the men were on top of me, they saw the young girl and the very act of being on top of me stole my innocence. Let me explain. I was still a little girl in my mind. It didn't matter how old I was.. My mind said I was a little girl. I was a girl who just wanted to be loved. I could stay that way until it was time to have sex. In some ways, I was split in two. There would always come the moment that the whore would have to take control and the little girl had to step aside.. The whore had to be in control because if she wasn't, I would have gone crazy. The little girl wanted to be held but the men wanted to be inside of her.

There is another way to look at it. It is a way that I don't want to see.

I chose to be the little girl because that is what the men wanted. You could not act your age. I was thirty and still acting like 15 because that is what men wanted. By then my innocence was gone . I still had to at innocent even though I knew the truth.

I remember a guy telling me that I was too lose .Really, I thought. He was talking about my female parts. For a moment I thought about getting some cream to tighten it up.

This is so deep. I don't know if I can go any farther. I can't tell everything.

I feel like you have to know the whore to see who I am

God , must I?

I have to ask God must I tell the whole story.

I will just say that I learned how to make the guy think I was tight.

When I look back at the image of what I did, I can't bear it

I just keep thinking. I gave them what they wanted.

It's Not About The Money

When you say whore, people think of money and material things. So, people think I sold my body for money and they might think it was all about the money but I wasn't the average whore. I wasn't getting paid. Yes, there were times that there was a price. But no one ever laid money on the pillow and I never put a price on having sex. I never made it about money.. I didn't put a price on my body.

If I said I took what I could get, it would be a lie. It was never about that. There were moments that it was sure lust and moments that it was love.

It was not what was in my mind or how I felt that made me a whore. It was the act itself.

Out Growing The Whore

So now you know.

The whore remained young and I grew up.

My youth didn't matter to me but to the whore , it did. How was she going to please the men if she was old and if no one saw her appealing.

Age waits for no one. I looked at myself in the mirror and I saw my body change. I was okay with it. I thought I was okay but in reality, I was losing apart of myself. I was losing my hair and my teeth and I could no longer take on the weight of the men. The whore hated it but me, I was glad.

You see, I didn't have to be the whore anymore. I convinced myself that because all this was happening to me, I no longer looked like the whore.

You could say that the whore was getting weakier.

I looked at my body and I could see that my body was tired of having a man between its thighs.

The question was asked how did the whore feel.

Who cares what she thought.

Was she sad?

I didn't think about her feelings. I just wanted her to let go

And God says

"But you are the one holding on"

And how can I not hold on to her?

That's what men only saw of me.

There was a time that I wanted to be sexy but I begged for a man to just see beauty.

A Piece Of Meat

There was this man in my life named Jay. Jay always looked at me from feet to my head . We were a couple , so it should not be a problem if he was looking at me, but I always felt some type of way when he did. Most women would have enjoyed it but I knew that look. He would look at me up and down I just felt like a piece of meat.

In those moments , I was learning to despise him. The sad part is , he didn't know why. My feeling of despise was growing on the inside because he looked at me like most men did. I use to love that look because it meant that I had it all together. But that look always said "I want to have sex with you" and sex is the nice word.

Men who look at you with lust only care about doing it. They don't care if it hurts and they always want you to take it. You know take all of them..

Don't say a word while they are on top of you or you on top of them.

Again you have a job to do.

Tell me ,how many men does it take to hate it when a man looks at you ?

I can't answer the question. I just know that there was a moment when being looked at did not feel so good.

That look, it use to put me immediately   in the mood to do something. Now it was just showing me that all you saw was sex.

You didn't see me. You saw the whore.

That look makes me think that that is all I am good for is sex.

I hear "But when God looks at you .."

It makes me think about the part in the Bible were it says beauty for ashes.

Beauty For Ashes

Ashes is waste . when something burns ,nothing is left but the ashes.

The whore represents ashes..

Maybe I am saying wrong. The ashes are me. Because I was destroyed. All that is left is ashes of my childhood; the ashes of who I was supposed to be.

Now if I give God the ashes, he will now give me beauty.

Instead of seeing myself as a whore, I can see myself beautiful .

I am thinking, man created the ashes but God can give me beauty for them.

65

It sounds like a fantasy because no matter how I want to see myself beautiful, I can't.

Beauty is what made them want me.

I tried to make sure that I did not become vain.

Yes I smiled when someone said I was beautiful and maybe I flirted but I wasn't going to let being beautiful drive me crazy

And as I say this, I hear..

You did let it drive you crazy

Why?

Because I slept with the men who said I was beautiful

And they are the ones who made me feel ugly.

Do I still feel ugly is the question.

A Message

The Holy Spirit talks to me from the word. I go to Isaiah 61 and read

The Spirit of the Sovereign Lord is on me, because the Lord has anointed me to proclaim good news to the poor.

(I have nothing. So I feel like I am poor. Without love, you are poor. So, God has good news for me.)

He has sent me to bind up the brokenhearted, to proclaim freedom for the captives and release from darkness for the prisoners,

(I just kept thinking about how no one loved me and how I felt captured by Satan. Sex is darkness for me.)

2 to proclaim the year of the Lord's favor and the day of vengeance of our God,

to comfort all who mourn,

(So God is going to bless me and deal with the ones who hurt me. He will comfort me. He will hold me.)

3   and provide for those who grieve in Zion—to bestow on them a crown of beauty instead of ashes,

.

(And there it is No one knew my tears or even worried about them but this said that God would provide for those who grieve. I was grieving for the innocence that I lost and even though I saw myself as unworthy, God would give me a crown of beauty instead of ashes)

the oil of joy instead of mourning, and a garment of praise instead of a spirit of despair. They will be called oaks of righteousness, a planting of the Lord   for the display of his splendor.

(He would give me joy where there were tears and I would have a praise instead of sadness and loneliness. No matter how many men you sleep with, you can still be lonely. The more men the lonelier you are..)

And I kept reading…..

They will rebuild the ancient ruins

and restore the places long devastated;

they will renew the ruined cities

that have been devastated for generations.

(God will rebuild me and restore my mind and my body. He will renew my innocence that has been destroyed over and over)

5 Strangers will shepherd your flocks;

foreigners will work your fields and vineyards.

6 And you will be called priests of the Lord,

you will be named ministers of our God.

(the whore doesn't have a name.it is a title. Now I am reading this and it says that you will be called priests. I didn't think this was a prophesy but I see that it was)

You will feed on the wealth of nations,

and in their riches you will boast.

7 Instead of your shame
you will receive a double portion, and instead of disgrace

you will rejoice in your inheritance. And so you will inherit a double portion in your land, and everlasting joy will be yours.

(That is me. I live in shame. No one knows how it feels to be the whore. . you can never be good enough)

8 "For I, the Lord, love justice;

I hate robbery and wrongdoing. In my faithfulness I will reward my people and make an everlasting covenant with them.

(I thought to myself that somebody needs this. And I kept reading.)

9 Their descendants will be known among the nations and their offspring among the peoples.

All who see them will acknowledge that they are a people the Lord has blessed."

10 I delight greatly in the Lord; my soul rejoices in my God.

For he has clothed me with garments of salvation and arrayed me in a robe of his righteousness,

as a bridegroom adorns his head like a priest, and as a bride adorns herself with her jewels.

11 For as the soil makes the sprout come up and a garden causes seeds to grow,

so the Sovereign Lord will make righteousness

and praise spring up before all nations.

I read it all the way to the end and I heard

Holy spirit, "You need this"

My Sword

Someone asked me a question.

What were you doing before this ?

I answered them "I was writing about God .

That's it. Satan did not want me to write about God. God was my first love.

In the spiritual realm ,my pen was my sword. Satan wanted to take God out of my life. With my pen I could fight Satan . all Moses had to do in the Bible was keep his hands up and he would win the war and now I see that all I had to was keep writing . I was supposed to learn my craft. I was supposed to be the master of it. But because life happens I chose man or man chose me.

And all I hear is "Pick up the pen, you are going to win wars with your pen"

Trying to Capture Love

I only loved two people in my whole life. My uncle and my first love

I say that because of how I loved them.

I have loved others but my love for my uncle was so great. I would have died for him. And the love for my first love. It was special and innocent.

All I can say is… ,that my uncle died. God took him from me. I could never forgive God for taking him. He didn't deserve to die. I turned my back on God for that reason alone. God wanted Satan to take me. He wanted me to be alone. He wanted me to suffer.

Someone asked the question. Did God want you to suffer or did he want to end the suffering for your uncle?

I never saw the suffering of my uncle. So I never thought that God took him because he was in pain. I just remember not saying goodbye and not wanting him to go.. I was upset because God took him and left me here.

I don't remember much about his illness. No one never told me and I never saw him sick. He wasn't supposed to die.

I had to realize that yes he was supposed to die .Life and death must happen. We don't get to say when

But it's just the fact that he loved me.

So, now I understand that what I have been trying to capture all of these years is that kind of love. I wanted my uncle and I tied that to men. That is why I could fix my mind to say sleeping with a man is love. So, when my uncle died, I met my first love and he became love to me and so and so on

Why Didn't I Tell My Uncle

I am trying to remember if my uncle was still alive when I was being touched. I want to say yes. But I know that by me saying yes could mess up my mind. If that's the case, I should be mad at him for not saving me. But how was he supposed to save me? I can't be mad because he didn't know. I should have told him.

If he had of known I am not sure what he would have done. I wonder would he have believed me. I wonder if he would have killed the person. Would he even try?

I Should Have Told My Sister

There were a lot of people that I could have told. I had a sister. Why didn't I tell her? I just keep thinking that I wasn't hurt by it . Maybe I wasn't even myself. I wonder would she even care. I think to myself that I could tell her now but what good would it do for her to know. It is too late for her to help me. She can't fix what they did to me. No, I can't say anything because of the expectation that I would have. I would want her to hug me and tell me that it is not my fault. I would want her to say that I did nothing wrong and it is going to be ok. That is too much to ask for. It is too late to ask for it.

Who Were You

Interrogator- Who were you when you were being touched ? Were you the whore or were you yourself?

I had to ask myself that question and be prepared to search for the answer.

After all of this time, I am still trying to figure it out.

Who am I?

It might have been just me. Maybe, I separated myself from within my mind to allow the men to do what they did to me.
.

I don't remember how I felt or the touch. So, did I just escape it in my mind?

I feel like, I was there, but I wasn't there. I was seeing it and it was happening to me but I wasn't feeling it.

And if that is the case; I have to wonder, were the angels taking on my pain. Were they feeling the touches to? But then I would be force to ask, why did I had to feel the other touches from the other men?

No! I don't want to remember.

To know who I was when I was being touched, I would have to remember what he felt like and smelled like . I don't want to remember. Time has passed by and I have forgotten. Why should I remember? I know that is where it began but that is not where it ended. I shouldn't remember.

I would have to ask myself, was I a whore then?

Again, I let the men touch me. I didn't say no. I don't remember crying about being touched .

A whore just let the men do what they are going to do. You better not fight. You accept the outcome.

The truth of the matter is, I wasn't lured into my room and I don't remember being offered anything. All I remember is what happened.

I don't know if I was the whore. I just remember being a kid.

Special

A lot of people will ask if the men made me feel special?
Which men?
The men who touched me when I was a kid?
I can't say. I thought it was just a game that we played I am not sure how I felt. They picked me and you know the rest. I guess I could say that in some way I would have to feel special. Many times I was alone and the men gave me attention. I want to say yes but I am not sure. I never thought of it as a great thing. I remember the kisses. He opened his mouth and I opened my mouth. I didn't run to the bathroom and brush my teeth and I don't remember smiling about it. I don't even remember what he said to me or if he said anything . I think I just thought this is what you do and that's it. I hate this feeling of ..even as a kid I didn't feel special.

Being Touched By God-Poem

Being touched by God is the greatest touch of all.
His touch will break the chains
And will break down walls.
It is the greatest feeling, nothing can compare.
Make you feel like you're flying in the atmosphere

Being touched by God

Many times people hear me talking about the men that have touched me but I want you to know that there are amazing touches. And those touches come from God.

He moves through you and in those touches are great joy.

I was eleven when God touched me. It was done through a song. The song is called Amazing Grace.

Now, I can see the song as a message from God. He had been keeping safe. I remember the song ministering to me . I was just sitting in a pew and the tears started falling. God was touching me. he was touching me and not the whore.

I found grace

I found grace when he touched me.

No matter how many times a man touched me, they could not beat God's touch and they might have had me for a moment but God has me for a life time.

I wish that I could hold on to that feeling but the whore only knows man.

I have to ask myself, if I can feel the touches of the men and be in spirit, then can the whore feel God?

It was bothering me.

Was not God's touch greater than the men.?

I told you yes. He touched me where no hands could go.

He touched my soul. It did not matter what my flesh was doing or how I felt, I knew God was touching my soul. Satan could do a lot of things but Satan could not deny God from touching me. He just couldn't.

My soul , my soul belonged to God but I knew Satan had my flesh.

Pulling You Out

This was a struggle. You can call it a war between me and myself.

I could hear

"Did you know that every time God touched you , he was trying to pull you out"

Me-Trying to pull me out. God is God. How does he try and not succeed?

"He did succeed but you went back. He was taking off chains and new ones were forming."

Me-So he just got tired of trying

"If I don't know anything about God I know this , he will not give up on you. He doesn't try to just try. He doesn't try. He succeeds. All things are possible with him."

Me-Then why am I not out

And I get this vision of a baby being born.. The woman is pushing and there are nurses everywhere. The doctor is sitting down and he is holding the baby's head.

He says "The head is out"

I get . your mind has to be free first then everything else.

Touched By Satan

Sometimes I have to ask myself the hard questions. Why ask when I should know the answer but I don't know the answers until I ask them to myself.

Has Satan ever touched me?

No one has ever asked that question

I could look at each man as Satan but they are not. I know that they are not.

So , has Satan touched me?

In the Bible God removed his hedge from Job so that Satan could touch him. He could do anything but take his life. God told Satan that Job would not curse him. So he could touch his life and everything that pertain to it but he would not curse him. No one really wants to admit that Satan can touch you but if he gets close enough......

I don't want to answer my own question and yet I need to answer it. But I don't want to because I would have to go back in my past and relive it. I am telling myself that there are somethings that I should just let go of. But, looking back can kill you.

"Only if you stay there"

I hear God saying that he wants to heal me.

I must finish this.

Satan came to me as evil. Then he showed himself as the devil.

Yes, he touched me.

.

I was fifteen , that's when Satan showed me who he really was. he touched by through being raped. I met this guy and his mother. We went to his house and he wanted sex. I slept with him. It was no love in it may be like .I don't claim him ,but my alter ego does. He was one of the whore's. well ,after he got what he wanted, he took me over to his sister and that is where I was going to live. Ione day I got mad at him and I did something that I should not have done. I spit in his face. He got so mad at me.

He took me to a bedroom and he started beating me. At that time, I wanted to die. I think in some way I felt like I should be dead. I believed no one loved me . so, I begged to die. I stopped begging once I realized that he would kill me. I don't understand why I changed my mind. I just did. It was a long drag out fight but once I said that I wanted to live , he stopped. Then he threated to kill me if I didn't have sex with him. He knew I was afraid. I looked into his eyes and I knew he would have killed me I just couldn't die in pain

So, I made up my mind to make him think that I was going to have sex with him. I had to think how to stall him. how was I going to get away. I went into the restroom. I think that I was looking for a window. I was hoping there was a window. He banged on the door and told me to come out. As I think about it.I remember his sister running out the house. It's crazy because if I think about, why is there no one to help you when you need help. People will let you get beaten, raped and even killed and they won't move to save you .

I was mad at her and I didn't know why. She could have saved me.

Then I hear," a mere man could not save you"

She was supposed to try.

Again I hear, "a mere man could not save you."

I yelled, "Why, why not?!"

The voice-Because they do not have enough strength to save you. Not everybody can go up against a giant. Before they can even go up against the giant, they first have to look at fear. A simple man cannot go up against a giant without God.

So.....

I had made peace with the fact that I was going to sleep with this man . I was coming out from the shower curtain.

Just remembering that is interesting

Because the bathroom is where I would always go and pray. Most people have a prayer closet or a prayer room but not me. Ever since I was child, I have prayed in the restroom . I don't know, it is just something about the bathroom. After being beaten, I looked for safety . I could have ran out of the house but I didn't. Why didn't I ? I can only guess that I didn't because he was watching me.

The bathroom was the only place and I remember him knocking on the door but that was the one place that he couldn't come into.

He yelled, "Come out !"

I was just about to when his mom came.in. You see, his sister ran to get his mom and when she came, she sent him away. He came back and there was no need to make me scared. I was already scared. He threatened to kill me and I knew he would do it. He told me not to make his sister nervous. With his very words, I was forced to lay down with him. He got what he wanted. Yes every touch was pure evil. Every touch was Satan.

Leaving Me In Satan Hands

How could God save me one minute and the next me leave me to be touched by Satan?

I think about it. I should have found somewhere else to go but I didn't. so I get raped

The voice-But you were left alive. This was a man that could kill you without thinking and he left you alive.

Me-But..But.

The voice-Do you wonder what would have happened if his sister had not ran to go get her mother? He was going to kill you that day but God saved you

I have been stuck on the rape when that was just a part of it. I was supposed to remember that I was saved.

God didn't let me die.

When he beat me , I didn't have any marks on me?

I remember feeling the hits but no, no marks and no, pain.

I look back over that day and I blame the whore for it. She slept with the guy and it had nothing to do with love. It was just straight sex. She didn't think about it. She just did it. I did it . I was the whore. I slept with him without thinking. I was so use to it by now. As I think about I realize one thing that I didn't say no when he raped me. Did I think I deserved it? I did spit in his face. That's what got him mad and Satan was just waiting for his chance to come out. I got beat down for spitting in his face and he raped me to show me that he was in control.

Making Up My Mind To Die

I let him beat me because I wanted to die but as he was beating me, I realized that I did not want to die like that.

I wanted to die but be at peace.

There were so many reasons why I did not want to live.

In the beginning it was because I didn't fit in. I was a mistake. Then it changed to no one loved me.

I think that death came first. I didn't belong. I was nine or ten when I thought about killing myself.

I wonder if felt like I was a mistake and unworthy because the boys had touched me. Maybe but I just can't imagine it. I didn't think that they did anything wrong.

Even know I question it. Did they do something wrong. In my subconscious maybe they did and I just didn't want to accept it.

No, sex didn't make me want to kill myself. I wanted to die because no one loved me. no one stayed. I t wasn't the act of sex. It was what happened after I had sex.

I keep hearing "Where did the thought come from?"

Why would I feel like death was the answer?

I told you that I had sex with these men and I did it for love. When they were done and didn't want me, the guilt of what I did with them and the idea that I wasn't good enough kept me wanting to die.

It was all tied together. After sex , I felt unclean. God could not have made a bigger mistake than me. I could write a list of all the people who did not love me.

Can I be dramatic?

I felt like nothing, very time I slept with a man and he didn't want me. He didn't want to keep me.

I realized that it was mostly because I didn't love myself.

No one ever shows you how to love yourself. When you are kid , you rely on your parents and family to teach you about love. If someone is always putting you down and insulting you, how are you going to know how to love yourself. You learn to hate yourself. You learn to hate your life.

The Test

One day I heard the Holy Spirit say "God says that he loves you"

I thought does he say that? Does he really?

I know, why would you question it?

I don't know what else to do. I have spent my whole life questioning God, myself and the people around me. I questioned if they loved me and the answer was no. How could they?

It was a no because that is what they showed me. Through my actions, I tested them and when they would fell the test, I knew that they didn't love me.

One guy that I was talking to had the nerve to say he loved me. well, after two weeks went by, I went over to his house and told him that I slept with another guy. I waited for his response. He questioned me about it but he didn't get angry then he wanted sex. He could have did anything but wanted sex because when he did that it changed how I looked at him.

He was no better than the rest of the guys. I looked at his actions as if he didn't care and I thought to myself that he would make it too easy to cheat on.

I wasn't afraid to tell him about any man because every time that I did was a test that he would fail. I wanted his reaction. I mean ,he should be angry but nope, that wasn't him.

Now I lied to him about sleeping with the guy and I wasn't ashamed of it. I had to test him. Later on I told him the truth. I think that I was destroying the relationship.

In my mind, I saw him as a man with no feelings .He wasn't committed to me. I wonder .was I the one who could not commit?

You know, I had sex with him before I told the truth and for the life of me, I do not know why. Maybe I did because he wanted me.

My mentality is I am going to give you what you want.

So I wasn't his girlfriend. I was his whore. He didn't lay down with someone who loved him. He had sex with the whore who had no attachments.

All I needed was one man that didn't say yes to having sex with me.

I tested him again and he failed again. This time I told him that we were breaking up. I was leaving for the last time. I wanted him to see what he would say or do. I wanted him to stop me and say that he loved me.

"Don't go anywhere"

Is what I wanted to hear. Instead I got

"well, we can have sex one last time'

What?

He didn't get it. Do you know what he did? Have sex with me, but yet he loved me.

Now every time I have sex with him, I am mad at him. I am mad at him for being like all the other men in my life.

Does he deserve it? I am not sure . I think, why shouldn't he pay for what he did .But I had sex with him. I could have said no and stopped it.

I won't accept that as an excuse .Again I gave him what he wanted, what they all wanted.

The Puzzle

I didn't see it until now.

That every time I did that, I gave them me.

I gave them a piece of me

The Holy spirit came to me and said,

Holy Spirit-When a puzzle is missing one piece, it is not whole. You are not whole.

I wasn't whole.

I remember thinking , if I am like a puzzle and I missing a piece, what piece am I missing?

Me-No, I am broken into so many pieces. I can't even count how many pieces I am in.

I never thought about it .

About how broken I have become. I did not start out being a whore. I liked boys but I didn't know all there was to know about sex. All I knew was the man is on top of the woman and they are naked. What the boys did to me was not sex. I have to tell the truth, I think that some form of sex was in my life and it might have affected me. I can't believe that I am admitting that. How could sex break so many pieces in my life? A touch might have started the breaking but there was more to it. I had the taste of sex and it changed me.

I know that I was young when this all started and I need for it to end. But it is so hard to end something that started so long ago.

The Holy spirit spoke to me again.

Holy Spirit-In the spiritual realm ,Satan put chains around you and dragged you to where he wanted you to go. But don't you see that your spirit fought and it continues to fight . Satan was trying to kill your spirit but he couldn't. So he took your flesh. You had sex because you were in pain and as you grew the pain grew. Your flesh was weak. Your mind was confused. You thought sex was a way to love.

86

Pain

And something amazing happened, my friend walked by and began to talk about his sister . He said that his sister was in a lot of pain. She has sickle cell anemia. He said that some pain she could tolerate because she had been through it before and then there were other pains that made her cry out as if she was dying.

I thought about her pain. Pain can mess with you in such a way that you don't even know who you are.

The Holy Spirit spoke

Holy spirit-That is what has happened to you. You have a great pain.

When you have a great pain, you go crazy. You become delirious and you can't think about anything else but the pain. Pain comes and goes. Sometimes it last for minute and sometimes it lasts for years.

When you are in pain, you don't want to get up. You want to sleep because your body is tired of hurting.

Even your brain gets tired . You can't even live or function when there is pain. You have episodes of when you can't take no more.

What he said made sense to me. I could relate to it. I understood it and I didn't know why I could .

 I would beg. 'Make it stop" when I couldn't take any more of the whore. You have to understand that the whore caused me pain. She was my pain and I was so stupid that I didn't see that she was. All I knew was the pain. Morphine couldn't help this pain. There was no drug that is known to man to help my pain. I learned that by the mere shock of the pain, there a chance that you could die. You can't think straight. I didn't know up from down . I was hurting and I didn't know where the pain was coming from. There were times when I wouldn't be thinking. There was so much pain that I didn't know when to be afraid. And when I slept with the men wasn't thinking at all. Sex made it hard for me to rest or relax. I couldn't relax until the job was done and I had to stay awake because the men would fall asleep and I was afraid of the dark.

All It Takes Is A Yes

Till this day, I still say yes to people and mean no. I said yes so many times to men and I meant no . I was in this hotel room with this guy and we were just about to do it. I said no but he made some off the wall comment and I was scared so I let him . I never thought of it as rape because he didn't force me. plus I went back to him again and again. Once he had sex with me, he had me. You know, he was married He had a whole wife. She even came up to my job. She was yelling and screaming. I remember her degrading my mother and mother had nothing to do with how I ended up. I was every name in the book. I deserved it but what could I do. I want to say that she didn't want to hear my side but a whore doesn't have a side. That day, my life was supposed to end. She pulled out a gun and threatened to shoot me, I told her that I wasn't scared and I said she shoot. She held the gun for a few moments and then she got in her car and left. I knew that she had every right to shoot me but God wouldn't let her. That same day I had to tell my boyfriend that I slept with another man. I told him everything and he choked me and then he held me. I realize now that he wasn't choking me, he was choking the whore and holding me.

In her defense, she was just doing what she knew to do.

Did she know that he was married?

I had to think about this question because what does that say about me if I say yes. It is better to say no. At least that would mean that there was some good in me

But who am I kidding.

At that stage in my life, there was no good. I don't even remember if I knew.

Did I ever sleep with a married man?

Yes, and I will leave it at that.

A Phone Call

God is showing me why this book needs to be written but I hate it because I don't want to see myself or feel hurt. I let the enemy get in as I was writing this. My friend called and all he said was that he talked to a friend. I assumed that it was a woman and it was. I didn't know how to take it. I got so angry because I loved him. I have been waiting for him and to think that he could chose to love someone else. I would have to deal with the fact that he gave up on me. He gave up on us. The words "But he had sex with me" will not work anymore. I want to use that and be mad at him but how can I be mad at him? He said that he wasn't going to try anymore .He said so many things that hurt me . I say that but did he really say so many things that hurt me or did I just hear what I wanted to? I remember him telling me that I needed to figure things out. He wanted me to figure out that he loved me in some way but he never realized that I wasn't going to figure it out. I wasn't going to believe it. You only got one chance to mess up with me; all you had to do was show me, that I was a whore and he did that. He wouldn't admit to it, but his actions ,they always showed it. Maybe it was me. I have to ask myself ,was it me?

Proof That I didn't Love him

If someone hurt you and told you that they didn't know how to love? Would you believe them and love them anyway? Would you at least try and how long would you try? I always tell people that I can love them for the way that they are but maybe it is not love. Maybe all that I have learned to do is accept what they are giving me and hate them while I accept. I don't like the thought of that.

God is telling me to face it.

All this time I have been the victim. I became the whore but first I was the victim. But I don't get a reward. See, the whore is always the victim because you don't know what she had to go through to be the whore. She has to (no exceptions)accept whatever the man wants. She is a tool for him to use and her mind , she has to get paid.

Interrogator-Why, when Jesus paid the price?

When Jesus paid the price stuck with me for a moment. What was I going to say to that? He did pay the price but it wasn't about that. Some people don't even know Jesus paid any price

Interrogator- But you did.

Yes, I knew that he paid a price for my sins but I wasn't willing to stop the sin.

Anyway, it is not about the price. It is remaining the victim. Because I was the whore I had that as excuse. Sleeping with men was my story. I wore as a badge. I told the story a million times. And that would have been okay except, I never stopped being the victim to what men had done to me. I say that because I still chose man. I could be with one man and go see another man with only a drop of guilt.

I wanted someone to make me stop. I wasn't going to make myself. I hated the life but again, I was used to it. I could be with someone else and tell my boyfriend about it to see if he even cared and if he did , it was problem. In my mind ,I would think that he didn't have the right to be upset. Then, he could flirt with a woman and I would take offense. Why? because he did it in my face.

Then I would use the phrase "You are like everybody else"

Interrogator-Which one is worse? He flirted and though it was wrong ,you went to another man's house? What makes you do it?

Me-Anything and everything. If I feel like I am not loved. Sometimes, I am just use to the person. Sometimes I can't help it.

Interrogator-Then why get mad for what men do to you? Why get mad at the men who loves you.

Me-Because if he loved me, he wouldn't do it. he shouldn't do it in my face and tell me about it.

Interrogator-So what he does, he does in front of you. Does it make sense to be mad at him when you use the excuse "I have to be honest' and you tell him that you were with another man?

I want to see his reaction. I want him to get angry.

Interrogator-And what, hit you or yell at you?

I want him to make me stop,

Holy Spirit-What you want is for him to hold you. You don't want him to leave you. You want him to put up with you and never get tired of trying to love you.

Me-He was supposed to understand.

Interrogator-what? You told him you loved him and your actions, they were not love. No, you don't want to be seen as a whore, you want to be seen as the victim but ..

I had stopped being the victim a long time ago. I can't claim it anymore. I am not the victim. I don't even want anyone to think that they made me the victim. A victim is weak and powerless.

Interrogator-Would you rather be seen as the whore?

That's what I was asking myself. The answer to that was no. I wanted someone to stop me when they couldn't .It's like I wanted to punish the people who loved me, when really I didn't

I understand that God is the only one who can stop me and I have to want to stop..

Can I say once again that I didn't know how to love. All I know is sex and to defend myself..

You Don't Listen

Many men said the same things that he said. I don't listen. I stopped listening when my mother would criticize me. I only heard negativity, so everything is negative. Then I think about sex and how the men said I was so good and how they mention how soft I was. How tight I was. I thought those were all good things. I wanted the men to feel something. They needed to feel me and say those things. I needed the kind words but over time they became dirty words. My friend didn't even know what he said that was so wrong. Maybe I misunderstood but I didn't want to tell him what I heard. I just wanted to be in pain about what I thought I heard and react to it. I wanted to pay him back for not wanting me. I told him that he took all my happiness and filled me up with sadness. He made the statement ,"I am glad I giving you something" because he was inspiring me and I told him that what he was giving me was torment.

Feel Nothing

I hurt his feelings but he hurt mine and I was learning not to care. I wish that I could stay in that mind set but no. I have to feel guilty because I was wrong. It has to be okay. Why would he love a whore? Okay it's not about that. I am just using her to feel sorry for myself. This is where I would call up someone and play the game. I'm going to get what I need to. I don't want to feel. I want to be numb and sex does that.

You see it changed over the years .I can no longer associate love with sex. It is not an emotional feeling. It is a physical one. I don't want to feel anything .I do not want to feel any emotions. If I must feel something, then let it be physical. You see when you are the whore, you can't feel. You must be without feeling. You won't survive if you have any emotions. In a way, it is to protect you. The enemy feeds off of emotions. He can take your spirit.

Doors Open

I was taken to a place that I had often visited. The place of another rape.

I was seventeen when I got raped again. The guy tried to kidnap me. I remember a door closing and his eyes turning red. I saw fire in his eyes. I knew something bad was about to happen. The guy took me to the room and raped me. Mama was on my lips. Mama is what I cried out.

. Then he decided to not let me go. I didn't say no. I just let it happened crying like a baby for my mother.

I don't want think about it but the Holy Spirit says to stay in the moment .

I don't want to.

Again the Holy Spirit says to stay there .

94

Stay in that moment.

What am I supposed to see?

The Holy Spirit-Did you see yourself as a whore while he was raping you?

Me-No, I became a child who needed their mother.

Holy spirit-Like I said the enemy was trying to destroy your spirit. He couldn't destroy it. So, in the spiritual realm there was always a battle going on .Satan wanted your soul.. He had to rape you. He wanted to control you .

Me-And he did he control me.

Holy spirit-No, your spirit cried out for God to be in control.

My rapist was going to kidnap me. I remembering him telling me that I was his and I was going with him.. I thought what was I going to do. I had to something. I had to get away. I could only think of one thing. I told him that I was hungry and he called someone to come. He said that I would eat in a little while. We waited and waited and the person never came

This is when the Holy spirit really began to talk to me .

Holy spirit-So what happened?

Me-He opened the door.

Holy Spirit-But you said that he closed all of the doors

Me-Yes, he closed the doors and windows.

Holy Spirit-and now you say that he opened the door.

Me-I said he had to open the door.

Then that's when it happened and I knew that my rapist didn't open the door .I know that it was God. The word says that God would open doors and he did.

One Moment

You would think that once the doors were open, I would run out but I couldn't run. He was too close to me and I was too scared to try. He had me. The moment he raped me, I was his. He had control. We walked to a restaurant and went in. He watched me. So he had put enough fear in me for me not to even look like something was wrong .

But

One moment was all I needed. When that moment came, I ran out of the door.

When it was happening I didn't realize what I had seen until I was questioned about it .

You see, I have told this story many of times and no one ever asked me

"Did you see God"

Then one day I was asked.

"Did you see God?"

Me-When?

"When you were in the restaurant"

Me-No….no I didn't.

"Yes, you did. God distracted your rapist , so you could get away."

Me-But why would God do that?

"Because he saw more than a whore"

Torn Apart

A few days ago the phrase torn apart kept coming into my mind.

I couldn't shake it. I kept trying to figure out the meaning of torn apart . what did it mean to be teared or should I say ripped opened. I have heard that phrase throughout my life and I never associated it with anything that I have been through and yet, it was in my mind.

But why?

I'm a dramatic writer and I have to write and pull you in. I want you to feel something . I have used the phrase before. I know to use it to describe rape but I never felt that way .

So, why was the phrase haunting me.

Then, God had me open my book. As soon as I opened it, I knew it wasn't finished. I was adding to it and correcting it. I thought I was done when I got to the part of crying for my mother. I remember that. I remember being ripped apart.

I wasn't the whore then. I wasn't even the seventeen year old who was experiencing it. I was … I was a child calling out for her mother, as she was being ripped open by a man.

It is like this man took a piece of sowed material and pulled each stitch apart. The material was me.

Violent Act

Violent sex
Pure rage at its best.
Associated with pain and tears.
Oh mama, I wish that you were here .
Satan gets a thrill,
As joy, he destroys.
And a part of life, he kills.
You do all you can to stay alive
You scream in silence to survive.
Violent sex
The pure need to take control
If you don't give it to me ,
I'll rape and take your soul
He'll rip you apart
Take your mind and your heart .
Leave you for dead.
Taking what he can get.
Making it where you never forget.

Control

I use to think of sex as special. The man was supposed to be on top of the woman and you kiss and hold each other but being raped has showed me something different. It is all about power. Yes, sometimes it is. It is about who has the control. Because I didn't have control during the rapes, made me want to have it when I was having sex. I climbed on top of the man and I made the rules. They couldn't touch me. they couldn't kiss me. They just had to lay there and I just did what I did. It took a lot of concentration. In my mind, I was saying "No, you don't get to tell me when to do it and what to do. I am in control". I wanted them to be weak. I'm the one in control and if they broke a rule then it would take me out of the moment. I would stop and if they wouldn't let me stop, I would change to a child.

I went with this married man to a hotel room knowing what he wanted. When we got there, he was ready for sex .I remember laying on the bed with him . I felt funny about being with him. There was a moment where I made up my mind to say no and there was a moment that I realize , he wasn't going to accept no. I had sex with him willingly in order not to get raped
You would think that I would have never saw that man again but I believe I did. I was never without blame.
Will you accept that I didn't know what else to do. The men had me once they had sex with me
I liked this man .I wrote him poetry but I wasn't in love with me and he wasn't in love with me. I just did what I knew to do.
I wonder did this start when I got raped or when I was molested?
I want to say that it is when I got raped because I was powerless in those moments.
I don't want to admit it but I was also powerless when I was being touched.
I want control now. When things are not in my control, I become anxious
God, I don't want control anymore.
I give it all to you.

When Did It Stop Being About Love

I don't know when it stopped being about love. I want to make it about one person and say that they affected me . I want to blame one person but to tell the truth overtime it stopped being about love and I don't know what it is about. Sex is supposed to beautiful and even a whore wants love. Sex is whatever you believe it is at the time you are doing it. Your partner is supposed to confirm that. You are supposed to feel safe. Sex was more about validation for and on those times when it was about love, I can smile but let's be honest most of the time it was sex. It was work and obligation.
I made myself believe that I was obligated to have sex. It just had to be that way.
I still used the excuse of love. Like I said I didn't want to admit that I was the whore.
At some point in my life I realized that love didn't matter to a man.
Most times they see women as their property. They feel like they are intitled to sex.
When a man makes it special for you , you would think that it is love but I now know that you will see love first before you even have sex with them.
If you sleep with a man on the first date, you haven't given them a chance to show you love.
And what about respect?

Many times ,the men lost respect for me because I had sex with them. For me it was the beginning of love for them it was proof that I was a whore.

I now know when it changed.

It changed with the more men that I slept with.

Love

I thought that I knew what love was but can a whore really know.

I thought, love was being loved by a man but I learned the hard way that love is being loved by God.

Once again the whore made the decision to have sex and my spirit is the one who got hurt.

I was so mad because I let man do it to me again. I had nothing after he was done.

I remember crying and God brought this to my remembrance.

Corinthians 13 says

 4 Love is patient, love is kind. It does not envy, it does not boast, it is not proud. 5 It does not dishonor others, it is not self-seeking, it is not easily angered, it keeps no record of wrongs. 6 Love does not delight in evil but rejoices with the truth. 7 It always protects, always trusts, always hopes, always perseveres.

8 Love never fails. But where there are prophecies, they will cease; where there are tongues, they will be stilled; where there is knowledge, it will pass away. 9 For we know in part and we prophesy in part, 10 but when completeness comes, what is in part disappears.

 11 When I was a child, I talked like a child, I thought like a child, I reasoned like a child. When I became a man, I put the ways of childhood behind me. 12 For now we see only a

reflection as in a mirror; then we shall see face to face. Now I know in part; then I shall know fully, even as I am fully known.

13 And now these three remain: faith, hope and love. But the greatest of these is love.

And God spoke to me "This is love"

 If this is not in your life then what do you really have.

The whore never knew what love was but in my spirit, I did.

I cried many times because I gave my body away. And in doing that, I called out to God just as many times and you know what? God never failed me.

Somehow, someway he came to me. He made it okay. I was wrong again and again. I chose man after man and I made mistake after mistake but Gd was still there.

At first, I didn't understand it ,but I get it, sex is just sex. It means nothing without love. You are supposed to see love at first sight. It does not say that love is easy. Love is mature

Love is an addiction and it is the greatest thing that you can have.

What Do You See

When all I could see was a whore, God saw more than a whore.

102

Why do I say that?

I say it because he had to see more than that .If he didn't, I wouldn't be here today. I wouldn't be the person that I am.

Do I think that he saw my spirit?

Here is what I will say/ My body belonged to Satan and my soul belonged to God.

I know that God saw my spirit. That part of me was not a mistake.

Were you the whore in church?

I never thought about being with a man in church. Sex wasn't on my mind.

My spirit was the strongest in church. When I was there my thoughts were only for God. Satan couldn't use me there we

If I looked at myself in church, would I see the whore?

I was always scared that a prophet would see me, for who I thought I was

The goal was never to admit it.

I prayed .

"God please don't let them see me. Don't show them who I am. I can't let them see me .

I was afraid that the whore would be seen but over the years God showed me that the whore could not be seen.

Why?

Because I loved God so much and you could only see the love I had for him. He was and is my love.

I continue to say it .I loved him. I just couldn't love myself because man took that.

I have looked in the mirror so many times and if you ask me what do I see. Well when I put on my make-up, I am beautiful. I am happy. I don't think about being the whore when I look at myself. I want to see something good.

One day I looking in the mirror and I heard

"what do you see?"

I said, "I don't know"

"You don't know because you can't get passed the image that you created for yourself. You have built a wall with this image "

I thought that the image was the clothes I wore but it was not about looking like a whore or playing the part.

What I saw was inside of me and it was based on her. I felt that I saw a whore. It was so clear to me.

"Oh God make me believe that I am beautiful.
Make me see that I am worthy."

I did not know that God was going to have to break down some walls to make me see what he saw in me.

You Tried It

I use to trust the Pastors at the church. I never saw them as
men. I mean they were men but men of God. They saw my
spirit. They saw my soul. If they saw something that wasn't
right, well they are supposed to cast it out. And help you
heal. They are the ones that you tell your secrets to. I have
learned that a minister and a pastor …even in God are still a
man.

One time I started talking to this preacher and I thought we
could have a relationship. He invited me late to his father's
church. He wanted me to go inside the church but he didn't
have the key. We stayed in his car and listened to his sermon
and then I was about to leave and he kissed me and at that
time I had not prepared myself to be the whore. So when he
kissed me unaware, I was a kid again being kissed again. I
felt so dirty and he knew I didn't like it. We stopped talking.
I don't remember hating him but I remember hating the way
I was.

I questioned God and myself. Why me. Why do they want
sex from me?

The last thing that I want to be is a hindrance.

Is it the clothes I wear

Or the way I do my hair

Is it my smile

Or maybe my eyes

Is it the dress that goes down to the floor

What tells you that I am whore.

What could it be?

If I needed any proof, that was proof that I was the whore. Men pick and choose who they think is easy. So, to that man I must have been easy. How could I deny being a whore when everyone else saw it?

Now I wonder if Satan set me up and wanted me to sleep with this pastor. Was it another test?

Pay Back

I will never understand why? why I was raped. I have learned to deal with it and understand that when I was getting raped, I wasn't the whore but I still felt like one. I could never convince myself that I was completely innocent. I was so scared of being raped that I fixed in my mind that all men was capable of rape. That is what Satan used against me. I was married and I loved my husband but one night I was in a deep sleep. I heard screams and it reminded me of rape. My husband approached me in my sleep . I know that I was telling him no. I thought he heard me. I was so tired that night that I couldn't fight him off. To be honest I don't think that I tried. I just kept saying no. When he was done, I was sure that he had raped me. as I am thinking about this, I am wondering if what I felt was being molested. Anyway, my mind said that I was raped. There was nothing that I could do about it now .it was done. He hurt me. So, I decided to pay him back. I decided to cheat on him. I thought it in my mind but I didn't think I would do it. Now at that time, I wasn't

106

going to church. God was in my heart but church wasn't. I think we just stopped one day and it was easier not to go back. Well, I met this man named Jason. He seemed friendly. He invited me to his church. I went first and I loved it. So I took my kids and my husband. We loved going to the church. No one told me what Jason really wanted from me.

Jason comes to me and tells me that we me and him could be good friends. Friends, that is the low key word for sex partners.

"Pay back" I agreed

I could say that I didn't know what I was doing but I did. My husband deserved it. I trusted him and he raped me. that's what I told myself.

God tried to warn me about this man but I didn't listen. So, I lied and cheated. I got away with murder . I was paying my husband back and hurting myself in the process. I wasn't even seeing myself as a whore and I didn't have any regrets because he deserved it. Let's just say I did the most. My actions told Jason I was a whore. Then things started to change. I began to fall in love with Jason. It was too late after that. See, now I wanted to spoil him. I made love wherever he said and in any way that he wanted.. I was his. He made it clear when he said that it was okay for me to be with my husband and with him but I couldn't be with no one else. I gave him all of me.

I know someone is questioning my walk with God. But I hope you would see that I needed God more than ever . In church I was praising God. That's the part people don't understand. I knew God and he meant everything to me. I praised him just because. He could take me away. Things would have been worse if I had stopped going to church.

Jason made me do things that I can't even say. I can't lie and say that I hated it. He was spending time with me and loving me. He made me happy. I stopped seeing it as payback

Why?

Because I loved the other man. Now I loved my husband to but.....

It was getting so hard to lie and cheat. I was in a fantasy and reality was trying to bust open. After a year of lying a cheating, I was living a double life and it was destroying me. I couldn't be with God and lay down with Jason. I think the hardest part was keeping it a secret. I couldn't be with my husband because Jason had me. It was catching up to me. One day I left my lingerie in the car .My husband saw it. He knew that it wasn't because of him.

I told Jason that I loved him and that I wanted to leave my husband.

I can't tell the rest

But God says I have to.

Jason wouldn't let me leave my husband. He said that he couldn't take me away from my family but he already did that.

That is when I knew that he didn't want me. He didn't respect me.

I was just someone to have sex with.

He wasn't going to leave his wife. Things changed after that.

And then.....

One More Man

I was on the edge of my world about to jump off, that's my way of saying I was going crazy. One more thing

Just one more. Really it was one more man. A guy that I had known came back into my life . One day, I went to go see him and all those feelings came back and I slept with him. I was already struggling with cheating on my husband.

I couldn't take anymore but Dean .He was back in my life and he reminded me of a time when there was no whore . See with Dean , I didn't see myself as a whore because he didn't see me as one. I slept with him because I loved him.

After we finished that's when I saw her and I couldn't deny that I was a whore.

Satan said, "If you sleep with three guys, you are a whore . I couldn't process that. So, I decided to run away. one night I left. I ran away from my husband and my kids to be with Dean. Even knowing that I was a woman with kids , I ran away.

I was so tormented by the whore that I knew if I had stayed, I would have had a breakdown and I would be in the hospital.

In that moment ,I wasn't thinking about my kids.. I couldn't think about them. If I thought about them, I probably would have stayed but I couldn't. I had to run away.

I didn't know it at the time, why I ran away but I know it now.

I was embarrassed and ashamed because of what I did. I couldn't face my kids.

When I met my first love, I always ran away to his house. I learned to hide in bushes and watch for my mother to see if she was headed in the same direction. I was good at running and hiding. I would make it to his house and just be with him. Then when he wasn't around anymore, I started running in school and it helped the pain go away. .

What pain?

The loss of my Uncle ,the hurt of my first love and the feeling of not being good enough and being alone. I would run away in order not to deal with anything and to feel safe.

I wonder if I was running away from being touched.

So I was a runaway slave. I was a slave to grief love (the illusion of), that I was nothing and being alone . I have learned that a runaway slave can run but they are still a slave. I wanted to be free. But here is the thing, I could be free of everything else but sex. It was a part of my life .it was who I had to become.

It was my deepest secret. It was my shame and it was away for me to survive.

God never intended for it to be that way . I know that.

Sometimes I have had to pray for God to take away the desire in my flesh.

Sometimes I have felt so dirty that I have put the blessing oil from the church in my bath water and I would drink the oil. I would pray for myself and cry in the water.

The water .. the water .without that blessing oil to cleanse me, to make it okay. I am not saying to make it okay for me to sleep with someone. No, but to make it okay for me to live with myself.

Reborn

I was baptized at the age of eleven and I didn't understand how important it was to be baptized didn't think of it as being reborn. I didn't really understand it. I thought of it as something to do. It was exciting to have my head dunked in the water. I remember practicing it in the tub. I was a little bit afraid of drowning. I was so happy that day .I got in the water and my head went under . I didn't drown and I felt like I had accomplished something. But I didn't know what it really meant to be baptized. The Bible says that we must be baptized by water and by spirit. By doing this we are reborn and we are no longer in flesh but we are in spirit. So, I am asking myself now. Is it possible that at the age of eleven I was reborn in spirit and at the age of eleven I was no longer a mistake? It's funny I don't see myself as a mistake anymore but I have to accept seeing the whore. I look at myself and I know that it was never about God. I loved God first. No matter what, I cannot deny God. I love him more than I love myself. The problem is me . it is me and Satan.

He gives me no peace. Because of that in my forties, I got baptized again and I prayed that the whore would be washed off of me. I wanted to get in the water and be a new person. I remember getting into the water and the pastor was praying . I think I started shaking. When I stepped out of the water, I did not feel like a whore.

I hear the Holy spirit say "The baby did not cry

See the doctors always want the baby to cry to get rid of residue in the lungs , nose or mouth. Because I did not cry the residue remained. I held everything inside of me when I am supposed to let it go.

Then I was supposed to eat .not what I had before but milk. I was a baby I needed spiritual milk. I was supposed to grow up in my salvation

I know now that I need to cry it all out. I am already reborn but the residue remains.

Filthy Rag

Do you know what I realized? A whore can never be clean. You can wash yourself over and over and still be dirty. I must admit it. I am a filthy rag. When I read Isaiah 64 :6

All of us have become like one who is unclean,

    and all our righteous acts are like filthy rags;

we all shrivel up like a leaf,

    and like the wind our sins sweep us away.

I got offended because I didn't want to see myself as a filthy rag.

That's not true . I was offended because I was one.

My pastor use to say the we are all filthy rags and I knew I was filthy but I didn't want anyone to say that I was.

It has taken this long for me to read Isaiah 64 :6 and know that it is true.

Nonmatter how much I loved God ,I laid with man and maybe there would not have been a problem if I was married or like some people say ,if it was one or two

But when I think of how many men it was, what can I say.

I know that I was swept away in (with) my sin.

I heard God say, "I can wash a filthy rag and make it clean."

Clean Enough

I use to like being in the tub or shower with a man. It was fun. It was wonderful. When you're with the man that you love, it is incredible.. It's all about you all.

But it's something different when you are just doing it with a man you like .Did I say. I guess you could like them but I am really talking about when it's all about lust.

I said it. I didn't want to because I have to see myself. I don't think that I ever thought about being clean, while I was in the shower with a man. We might have washed each other

113

off but it was about sex. I never thought that being with a man in the water was dirty.

I started taking showers with men, when I was fifteen years old. I was in the shower and the man came in the shower with me. I knew what he wanted. By that time , I knew what men wanted from me. I let him do what he was going to do and when it was over I got out of the shower.

There was no feeling. So, I didn't feel some type away. I didn't even know what I was doing. I just did it. Then time passed by and I saw being in the shower with a man fun and exciting. I know, it always leads up to sex but isn't that the point?

I wish I knew then what I know now. Years went by in my life and the memory of taking a shower with a man just makes me feel dirty.
Let's just say that you can be in a shower and still come out just as dirty as you were.
I never saw myself as the women who needed to take a shower after their rape. I was never that woman. I won't lie, there were times when taking a shower with a man seemed like a good thing. It was romantic. But over the course of time, it was just a shower and instead of feeling clean, I felt like I had been in the mud. There is no way that you can sleep with man after man and still remain clean . No matter , how many showers you take with them, you can't be clean

A whore gets use to it; smelling them , accepting the smell to a degree that it no longer bothers them. What happens when you get tired? No matter how many showers you take or how much soap that you use, you can't get the smell off of you .
I never thought about washing the smell off. I took showers but one day I couldn't stop feeling unclean. I could smell those men on me , I was so tired of the smell that I took

blessing oil and I poured it all over me. I washed every part of me ,including my hair.

I prayed to God to make it stop. I even drunk the oil. I just thought that I needed to get clean for God. I wanted to be clean .

I heard the enemy say "Just because you take a shower doesn't change you from being a whore. You can't wash it off." I realize that you can wash off the sweat but you can't wash away the memory.

The Holy spirit says, "That's what needs to be clean"

And not just clean but cleansed.

I have never been shy or scared in the shower. But how can I take another shower with a man again and not feel disgusted.? How can I take a shower with my husband and feel that it okay.

Will I feel pure and Holy or will I feel like a whore?

Satan will say that you can never be clean. When satan has you, he wants you dirty. He wants you feel that way and he will never clean you. He'll never give you that much respect. When you are in your sin, he's your master.

When it comes to a whore, he's your pimp. I

I see this image of a woman with a towel. She is taking the towel and wiping herself. It is so clear.

I ask God

"Why must I see this vision?

He says because satan will not clean you.

He will not anoint your head. He only wants you clean enough to do what you do.

The whore has no time to take a bath. She only has time to clean between her legs and wipe underneath her arms , put on perfume , a wig and brush her teeth(that's a maybe)

You will never be clean being the whore

Leaving Me Dirty

I had a relationship with one guy and I remember him spilling himself on me He would put himself between my body parts. He would get to that moment and do what he would do. It hated it when he did it . I would think how he must have hated me you see, he left me nasty and never cleaned me up. Every time he did that, I felt like I was a kid getting molested. He waited 'till I was sleep and he did it I couldn't help it, I thought of him as monster.

As he was getting a thrill, I would say in my mind this is how he did it .This is how he molested young girls.

Then, he would get up, he would clean himself and not even hand me a towel…In that moment , I was no longer a child but a whore.

I didn't want to see myself that way but he made me look at myself that way.

Out of all people. I loved him and he made me see myself that way. He could tell me no different. His "I love you" meant nothing. I finally decided to leave him. Years went by when I saw him again and he apologized to me and he wanted me to understand that he thought I was with other men.

I forgave him but I couldn't stop thinking that I could have accepted sex from him. But what he did to me made it hard to accept myself.. he made me feel like trash.

He couldn't tell me no different. That's what you do to whores.

If that wasn't enough, I remember this guy spitting on me. He was trying to get me where it would be easy to enter inside of me .. It was so nasty.

In my mind, I was upset .that just let me know he didn't care but I did like I always did. I went with the flow. I couldn't let it bother me.

Why did I continue?

What was my reasoning when it bothered me so much.

He defined me in that moment as a whore. He said he loved me but we had broken up. I was still trying to be with him.

Same old same.my story never changes. I remember fighting with him and telling him how he should not have done that .

I don't even remember what he said .

Does it matter?

No because as usual, I let him.

So if he saw me as a whore, I was a whore.

The Hair

One day, I was combing my hair and I began to think about the times I wore long hair and ended up in bed with a man. Long hair was the thing to have . You learn that men like to pull it. I thought about how I let the men grab my hair and how I gave all of my energy to the man, that my hair would be soaking wet. Thinking about it made me touch my head and think …now my hair is thinning. I wasted my hair on men. Someone asked me did I do my hair solely to be in bed with a man? I felt ,if I answered the question with a yes, I would be a whore. If I said no, I was safe. I answered it truthfully . We all prepare to be beautiful for the man that we love. We get dressed up for the first date .not in hopes of sleeping with a person but in hopes of love. For a moment , I wanted to blame my hair getting thin on the fact that I used it while sleeping with men. Sometimes, I wear wigs to change my look and for most women that would be okay but for me, it is always a question. A friend of mine wanted to know if I played the part, which means did I wear the wig for the sake of sex .It was easy for me to tell them no. Yes, I wore braids but a wig…no. I wasn't trying to portray the whore. I wasn't trying to be something I wasn't

I had to be what they wanted me to be in order to get attention and love. I would not have done anything but everyone knows that you have to be beautiful. Even the Bible says that a woman's hair is her crown and glory
It is funny because I would gladly cut all my hair off and never wear a wig for love.

Brushing My Teeth

Remember you'll never be clean. There was always a chance that I would look in the mirror and be reminded of her.

One day I was just brushing my teeth and thought about all the men that I had kissed. I was sick with the thought. I could remember their taste. You don't forget nothing .

When you're in the act, you are not thinking but when you have time to really put thought into it your actions. I had to brush my teeth.

A whore will rush their teeth enough to get by. Two minutes top. They are in a rush. I had to clean my whole mouth. I brushed my tongue. I had to use a special mouthwash.

The dentist tells me that bacteria covers my mouth and I will lose my teeth. I have to wonder is it because of my actions.

I know it is not but I still wonder and I hear God telling me that he will give me a new smile.

Escaping The Whore

I could never escape the whore.

But what does God see me as?
I asked myself many times ? There were times that I was in my own skin and felt like nothing. There were times that I was with family and felt like I didn't exist but when I was with a man I was baby.
Baby too many times. I was precious

Precious enough to have a man lay on top of me.
I was somebody. Yes! I was good.

Then as I grew up, I realized that being with a man was habit
and it did not make me special. I was nothing. It was the
moments that I was not with a man that made me something.
Anytime I allowed myself to be in God's presence, I was
something but I couldn't allow myself to hold on to that.
Always, someone would come along and remind me of who
I was. Women they reminded me that I was no more than a
slave. Men reminded that I was no more than a way for them
to gratify their selves.
No one showed me who I was supposed to be. I had to learn
on my own.
One guy actually decided to relieve his DNA on my body.
And I just accepted what he did. I wasn't even thinking
about it. I was in my zone . See, I was the whore. I was
letting him do what he wanted. A good girl does not
complain. You just do what they want and accept it. You are
in the moment and you are there to make them feel good.
I have never thought it, but it was important to me to make
them feel good. It was what I did right.
I thrived on affirmations "you're doing good", "Great job" I
needed to know that I was doing something right.

So when men would say "Oh, you feel good" that made me
smile. I thought God made me this way to please men and
because I thought that, I could keep going until we were
done. No that it not the truth. I knew I was God's mistake
and satan was using me. But I was good at it and that is
what I held on to.
A man never said I was crazy while I was on top of him. As
I got older, I saw the whore for who she was and I remember
crying . The whore had a soul .She was imaginary and I was

real. She had feelings. I had learned to hate myself and hate the men.

There was this man that I was dating . I liked him and he liked me. We made love. I am not sure if it was even love and he released himself on me. I went off on him because I'm not dirt. He said he was sorry but there was no coming back from that. I kept thinking that he should have known better. I realize a man will try you to see what he can get away with.

See by that time I was tired of letting and man get thrill by making me feel nasty. I was no longer young and naive was getting tired of accepting what man was giving me.

I didn't want to please them anymore and love wasn't enough.

A man who loves you treats you special.
They respect your body.
I told him that releasing himself on me was like someone throwing up on you and there is no respect in it .
Once I thought when a man releases his pressure inside of you , it was a good thing. Now I have learned to despise it. And if I get any joy out of it, I hate myself when it is over.

Get Their Hands Off

For years the whore tried to exist, but my spirit was fighting. The both of them could not have power. One had to be in control. So one day I was at church and I was depressed. My boyfriend, his touches did not feel good anymore. I didn't want him touching me .It made me think about the men who touched me. My body remembered them. In the spiritual realm these hands were all over me touching me. All I kept thinking was that I wanted their hands off of me.

Please get them off of me!

I thought today I am going to get their hands off of me .

I believe that I was already running around the church. My pastor, she had told everybody to run.

Normally, I would not have gotten up because I believed that in order to run around the church, you had to be in the spirit. So why should I run?

but two weeks earlier, my pastor said to me that if someone says run, you should do it. There was a reason for it. She said that you didn't have to be caught up in the spirit. You just needed to do it .

now, I told you that I was a runaway. I was good at it but on that day even though my flesh was moving, it was not my flesh running. In the spiritual realm ,my spirit also has the ability to run

I remember sitting in the church feeling uncomfortable. I had these hands on me. I wasn't thinking about them at the time. So, my pastor was preaching and the holy spirit said "when she says run, you go" I said yes. So the pastor said something like "Run" and I started running. I didn't feel nothing at first but his hands upon me. I kept running and the more that I kept running the more I kept thinking, I am going to get these hands off of me. I wasn't going to stop until I did.

So, I kept running but it wasn't me running. On that day it was my spirit running and my spirit wasn't running away from something. My spirit was running to freedom. I kept running and running until I couldn't feel those hands upon me.

At some point in the moment of me running , I passed out and I heard the pastor speaking and I felt the oil on me. When I got up from the floor. I knew that those hands were gone.

But the whore still remained. After all that happened, I still couldn't get rid of her. I don't think that I thought about it. I was just glad that I was free from the hands.

Letting Go

The time came when I realized I needed to leave the man that I had loved with all my heart. We had so many issues . I loved him for over thirty years. I could not let go of that love because that is all I knew as love. He was my soul mate. Because I felt that way I allowed him to hurt me and I hurt him. There was no leaving. Then one day, I met a man and I knew he was from God. I prayed to find a man like him. All I had to do was let go of the man that I was living with and wait to sleep with the man that God choice for me. Two things that I did not do. So I lost everything. I did not get the blessing that God had for me.

I see now that I didn't want to lose any man in my life. I had to hold on to them. I held on to them even when I was with other men. I held on to them even when I didn't see them anymore. At this moment in my life, I understand the word strong hold means. It is a strong hold that you cannot let go.

You either learn to accept it or you fight to let it go. There were some men that I gave power to and because they had power , I couldn't let go of them. Yes, their hold was so strong.

I think of the Israel people in the Bible. The moment that they were set free from slavery, some wanted to go back. Why? Because Egypt was a place that they had known all of their lives. They had got used to it. They hated it because they cried out. They wanted to leave but yet their minds wouldn't let go of it. A strong hold is when that that is holding you(whatever it is) has every part of you

Sex was my strong hold. It wasn't just the act of it. It was the after effect of it. Sex is supposed to be something you share with a person that you love. You can't see it as just fun. That one person that you get with could open a door. They could attach themselves to you the first time that you have sex with them. They could leave you and you will still be attached to them.

One day a woman told me to pray to remove the strong holds in my life . I prayed and Prayed

"Remove it God. Remove it from every part of my mind, my body, my heart and soul"

I wanted to let it go. I was praying to let the strong hold with the man go but not the strong hold that the whore had.

How do you let go of something that has been with you all of your life?

Everybody Knows Who You Are

Even loving someone can be a very big strong hold. When you love someone so hard , you will allow them to hurt you. When a men can play with your emotions , you have given them power. One guy had the ability to make me feel so tiny. He knew who I was or should I say that he knew the whore. He knew my problems with her. He knew how I felt about being her. Again, the whore was a secret. He wouldn't let her be a secret. I was the whore. He implied it. He implied that I was a whore and because he did it publicly, I believe that opened a door for his friends.

I know men will try but when you have lived the life that I have , you see a "come on" as a confirmation that you are a whore.

One day, this guy named Stan knocked on my door and said that he wanted to come in. He wanted me. He was a nephew of my boyfriend. I didn't know what to say. I never knew what to say. So I told him to come back and when he came back, I didn't answer the door. I prayed to God that he would go away and guess what? He did and he never came back. I wondered why did he come to my door? What had I did to him to say I was a whore? Then I thought that my boyfriend set me up. Maybe, he was using Stan to test me; to see if I would be so dirty to mess with his family.

But I wasn't the whore. I had rules. I wasn't going to sleep with a brother or any family. Friends were even off limits.

I would not be with his family whether we were together or not and friends, I did it twice. But me and the guy wasn't together.

It's funny because I ran into that situation a lot. One time it was a brother. He waited till his brother was sleep and when he knew that I was going to the restroom, he had all his stuff out. I thought that I was going crazy. I told myself that I was imagining it . Then the next day, he showed me who he thought I was. He showed me his body parts. He thought I would do something with him, but I was unphased by it.I just over looked him. Even then I could not say "Leave me the hell alone"

I just pretended not to see it.

Do I blame the men in my life? No. Just like I am telling this story to the world. I told it to them. I have written about it so many times. Men will see what they want to. I hate that I have to tell it because I know that somebody will say her name "the Whore" but I have to tell it.

God let me see, he just let me know that there were times when my spirit had more control than the whore.

You see, I didn't sleep with the brother .He tried it more than once, but I didn't

And the brother began to respect me.

Just Enough

One day the Holy Spirit came to me and said that no man could be inside of me. So I took it as, they could do everything else but have sex with me. I was going over to Dennis house every day. He would feed me and I would sleep in his bed. We were not having sex but I was laying with him. You would think that it would be okay but no. I

126

felt like the whore for just laying with him . To tell the truth ,
I was living with another man named Mo. I believed that Mo
loved me and I loved him but Dennis ..we were close.

One night I kept thinking how I let Dennis touch me and
how I let him be close to me. Often I asked myself, "Why
are you over here?". And when things got heated , I would
remind myself that I could not let him inside of me. I felt
like I was passing the test . I made myself believe it but my
soul would not line up with my mind. It was still wrong .
How can I say that? Because if it was right, I wouldn't feel
so ashamed. I would not have felt so wrong.

Many times I left Dennis house and went back home. Mo
never knew. I didn't know how to tell him. When I couldn't
take it anymore, I told his friend that I was moving and I
would be with Dennis. He told Mo and instead of telling him
the right way I attacked him. I was trying to push him away.
I told him that he could never be Dennis. Dennis was better
than him. I was going back to Dennis. By doing that, I got to
see his pain. I hurt him .why? Because I didn't know how to
be loved. I never went back with Dennis. We remained
friends but I couldn't take the chance to be anything more. I
think about what Mo's pain looked like and I wonder, if his
pain looked like that, what did God's pain look like?

I won't let Mo get off so easy because he took one moment
in time to have sex with me and not feel anything. He got
what he wanted. He paid me back by making me feel like a
whore.

You Are Still Being Molested

I had a friend who constantly wanted to give me hugs and touch me on my shoulders. I told him that I did not like it but he did it anyway. I said stop in so many ways without actually saying stop. I thought that he would get the hint but no he didn't. Instead he started giving me things and making me feel good. Because of that I let him hug me. I never saw it as a bad thing but I was giving him what he wanted.

What is wrong with a hug?

For me, everything.

See, I knew that he was testing me to see what I would give up. He wanted to know how far he would have to go to get what he wanted. Maybe he wanted friendship. Maybe he wanted to be a good friend but I know he wanted sex. He said it and his actions showed it. I wasn't going to do nothing with him . I just did what I normally did. I just smiled and changed the subject. I was being molested. I didn't fight back.

They say that when you are being molested the person will groom you. They will test you over and over again to see what they can get away with. It can be as innocent as giving you a piece of candy. They have to establish trust with you.

He was grooming me.

I hear the Holy spirit.

Holy spirit-That's how he does it. That's how Satan does it.

Satan will come as a friend. He will gain your trust. He will give you things and take what he wants. You won't know you are being molested until you are molested. Then, you are destroyed and you are his.

I thought that I had gotten over it.I wasn't even thinking about being molested. Until, something happen. One day a lady asked me to do something and it was something that I did not want to do. In my mind, I was saying no but when you can't say no, it's a yes. I was being forced to do something that I didn't want to do. I felt like I had to say yes. After I said yes, I don't know what happened. I just got really scared and I hid under the table for a few minutes

I heard the Holy Spirit say, "You are still being molested"

But how? After all of this time. How was I still being molested ? Besides I wasn't a kid .Only kids get molested and I knew that I wasn't being raped.

And the Holy spirit said again, "You are still being molested."

The Holy Spirit showed me that the times where I should and wanted to say no, I was saying yes and hating it and hating myself for saying yes. I even hated the outcome of it. I would be feeling sick and dirty. I can't even say dirty. It is better to say numb.

The Bible says that we should do things out of love and that your yes should be a yes and your no should be a no.

I had to understand that it is okay to say no.

I don't mean saying no to God but to people.

I had to learn that it is being molested when people are asking you to do something and you are trying to say no but they won't accept it. You finally give in but you are not feeling right about the yes you gave. You feel like you have been compromised.

No Touch Zone

My boyfriend touched me in a no touch zone.

What is a no touch zone?

It is a place on my body that reminds me of being raped.

When I am touched there all I see is the rapist and all that I can feel is the rapist touch. When my boyfriend touches me there, I forget who he is . I forget that I love him.

There are times that I hate him for touching me. Because my vision is impaired and I see him as a rapist. He doesn't understand. So there are moments that I have to tell him no, don't touch me there.

I have to tell him more than once. When he doesn't listen and continues to touch me , I feel that I must let him.

By force, I must let him. And when I do that , all I can tell myself is that he is raping me. My boyfriend doesn't hear my screams because I am screaming on the inside. I am begging him to stop, but it is all done in my mind.

There are times, when I can stop him and make him realize that the person he is touching does not remember who he is. I just want him to hold me and kiss me. I want his help to remember who he is .And when helps me to remember him, I am safe.

130

He tells me that he doesn't want to remind me of my rapist. He doesn't want to remind me that I was a victim. But I feel that he has no choice but to remind me. There are moments that he can touch me there.

Why shouldn't he be able to touch me anywhere on my body? Sometimes, I do not feel anything but his touch. Then there are the moments where I can't let him touch me where rapist have been.

I know I said that I was free from the touches and yes I am but there is this every now and again.

I had to ask myself ,if he knows not to touch me there and I have told him many times not to, why does he do it over and over. Does he forget or is the enemy using him?

The Nightmare Verses Reality

See, everything that had something to do with sex was the whore and I could be her for moments at a time, but it never lasted. Sooner or later, reality had to emerge. I could take myself to a place and become her but it never lasted because sooner or later I had to remember who I was.

I laid in my boyfriend's bed. Let me correct that Jerry wasn't my boyfriend. I had known him along time but we were never a couple. I think that was the problem .I loved him but because of the life that I had lived, I didn't know how to show it. Sometimes me and the whore would get mixed up. Sometimes my love would turn into regret. When it came to him, there was always regret. He could be my friend one minute and my enemy the next. I want to say that he never knew it but he did. I just felt like he didn't care. He didn't mind having sex with her. He was like everybody else . I think that he loved me but I was never sure. Did he want me or did he want the whore? One night, I was laying down with him and my hands were on him. I was doing what I knew to do. I was giving him pleasure. In my mind I was saying "Let me just do this and please him. I had to fix my mind to do it.I stop being me and I became her . But it was getting harder to remain her. I was struggling with who she was and with who I was. Normally I didn't have a problem being naked but on this night I took the covers and covered up my whole body.

(I am reminded of Adam and Eve hiding from God because they knew they were naked.)

The only thing that was left out in the open was my hand.

I said to myself that I could do this, please him but there was one rule, I couldn't be touched. As I continued touching him ,something was happening. I tried to remain in the moment and be her but reality was coming out. He got excited. He removed the covers off of me and reality was forced to come out. He got on top of me . He wasn't himself. I had never seen him loose control. I couldn't let him do it. I couldn't let him have sex with me. And if I did, I knew that I would see it as rape. I could have said nothing and let him do what all the others had done to me but no. That's what I yelled. No! he came to his senses and he got of me . I was shook and my anxiety was up. I laid on him and it only took a second for him to push me off of him.

I thought about all the other times that I had laid on him. He didn't have a problem with it after we had sex.

Then I realized something was different. We didn't have sex and he was in a mood because I said no. He didn't want me. He wanted the woman that would have sex with him. But why? He saw me having an anxiety attack and he wouldn't make me feel better. Then, he turned his back on me. It took all my strength to realize that ,that is the way he slept. I kept telling myself that I shouldn't be mad but I was. He wanted the whore but I couldn't be her.

The next morning, it all came out. He blamed me for us not being together

He told me that it was my fault and all of my problems.

Where was the compassion?

There was no. we will work it out. I was too damaged for that.

And for me, there was no reset button.

I realized by saying no to him gave my spirit strength and I realized that I could no longer give the whore life, control, and etc.....

He Wanted Her

He was use to her. Tell me ,how could he want her and not me. What was wrong with me? Many times I was her .And it was easy to be her but it started to get hard. She couldn't come out like she use to. To be honest, I was tired of her and he chose her. I had to see that he wanted her and the only time he wanted me is when she had did what he wanted.

I think about when we first met. He saw me and he wanted me but it was over once he met her. She was more important. Maybe I made her that way. I lived as her for such a long time. Sometimes I wasn't even aware of when she would come out. I just knew that she was out. So I guess I let him see her and he got use to her and it made sense, that even if he didn't want me, he wanted her.
It's not fair. They could lust after her and never love her and me...me; they wanted nothing. They didn't even want to love me. Once they saw the whore, I didn't matter.
I could blame myself for it and I do because I let the whore destroy my blessings. She took from me and they took from me.
Do you know how hard it is not to be crazy. Not to be me. No one asked why I was like I was. I did anything to be liked. I did anything for attention and no one asked why. They put the title crazy on me. I wonder if I was acting out because I had no one or because I couldn't tell? Was it all about being molested. God took my uncle from me and he was the only one who loved me. I know that it isn't true but you try telling a ten year old that. I was safe in my uncle's lap. My mother often said I could not keep my mouth closed about anything but I kept the biggest secret, until now.

Deal With It

A whore... I don't even want to say the word whore. It makes me sick . I want to spit it out of my mouth .

"Purge me oh Lord"

134

I understand the phrase now .

I want to throw it up and get it out. It is a sickness to me..

Maybe writing this book is a way to let it out.

Every whore has a coping skill. I have talked about it before.

It's not what gets you in the mood, it is what keeps you in the mood. Some people just lay there and stair into space dreaming about a better life.

Some people go numb and hide their tears. You do that when you are raped. You take it all in

While the man is on top of them , taking from them, some whores are being filled with hate.

Maybe in the beginning you were raped. The first time he took it but as I have mentioned, the second time you earn not to fight

The whore does not get a chance to ever say no.

"Deal with it."

"Deal with it."

When I said it the first time, I was thinking deal with what the man does to you but I felt something touch me and push my stomach and the second meant deal with what happened to you.

It all has to come out.

Whatever I touch..every man that I touched.

I can't even washed my hands enough.

I wanted their hands off of me but my hands. I had to learn where to touch them to be the most effective. I had to learn how to touch them. I had to learn their body with my eyes clothes. How does a blind person see? Through touch. I couldn't …

Then the phone rings and it is a blind person. He called because he got a voice message to call this number. Now it was a scam but what he said was God

He said he was blind and because he could not see he depends on touch. He cannot look at a number to see who calls, he just has to pick up the phone.

Deal with it

He spoke to me

This man said he was beaten by his step dad in order to learn his time tables. Whenever he got an answer wrong, he got hit over and over again

It touched me because I was a bruised through sex. Every unclean man who entered my body was hit to my spirit.

I had to get it right. I had to .

The way they pushed up on me. And the way they positioned themselves on me No matter how uncomfortable it was, I with stood it. I took it. If I got anything wrong I wasn't doing my job.

It wasn't them beating me, this was a spiritual fight. Satan was the a bruiser. I have scars to prove it. The only problem is, you can't take a picture of my soul.

Why Be Afraid

The man said that one day his father bet him until he could feel no pain and his spirit left his body. In that moment he learned not to be afraid . He learned to stand up to him. He said ,"If you have experienced all the evil of the world , why be afraid. He said, " I am not afraid of no man .I never have fear because God is there.

I was never afraid of satan. I was afraid of not being loved. I still cry over my uncle because he loved me.

Again , do I think he would of protected me. I don't know but he was supposed to be there. He was supposed to stay with me.

He was supposed to protect me. My brother who died was supposed to protect me.

But they didn't.

The man reminded me that God was there.

The reason that I can speak now is because I am no longer afraid. What can a man do to me? Nothing.

Your Private Dancer

The other day, Tina Turner was singing "I'm Your Private Dancer" and I begin to think how music plays a very important part in a whore's life. For me, I lost my self-respect in a song. Music made all the difference in how I performed. I couldn't think about what I was doing, so music drowned everything out. I had to have music. I couldn't dance without it. I could disappear in a song and the whore could show herself. She was the dancer.. She was the one who stripped for a living. It wasn't me. She took her clothes off for them. It was all part of the dance.

Part of Tina Turner's song says "dancer for money"

The whore isn't a prostitute. She is not selling herself. She takes what she can get. Love was supposed to be the payment. She never got what she was worth.

Prostitutes get paid more .They have a set price and a call girl, they are high class

They all do the dance in secret but the cost is greater.

You never get paid enough to be in the dance..

Pray For Her

You know what is funny? I feel sorry for her. She was born this way. She was born the very first time that I was touched by a man. How can I stay mad at her. Whatever she did to me I should forgive her.

God forgive her for all the things she has done.

God take away her pain. Heal her from the inside to the outside. Let her know that you are there for her.

God show her that she is beautiful in your sight.

Shine a light on her God that the whole world can see. Only you can release the chains God and set her free and when you set her free You set me free.

Oh God! We need you now! Move in her God. Move through her God .

Change her and let her be a witness to who you are. Let her see herself through your eyes , God

In Jesus name, I pray Amen

God Will Deal With You

Every man has been my enemy. I know this. Once they show me who they are they become someone that I have to fight against. All they have to do is make one mistake.

I was with this guy for a while and I thought he was wonderful Satan was using him to destroy me. See, sex was like a drug to me. There was no saying no to it. Now I mention how I learned a man but in return, they learned me and this guy knew my body. He knew her. That's what made him my enemy. Once we did it ,respect was gone. He only knew sex. I could tell. So he could kiss me and touch me. I thought it feels so good but to me it was more of lust than love. I kept falling into Satan trap. So one day I decided to speak some things as he tried to have sex with me. I knew he was going to succeed but I wasn't going to let him win.

God deal with him.

You deal with because I can't.

God deal with him .

Make him see that what he is doing wrong.

Make it where he can't rest.

There is no peace for him.

God deal with him.

Deal with him in a way that he will know who I am to you.

He can't make me go there.

He can't turn me around.

God deal with him. Make him think before he even desires me.

If he hurts me, deal with him.

If he causes me any pain deal with him

If he makes me cry, deal with him God.

I Don't Wanna Cry Anymore

I have cried so many times over the same man and man after man. When things didn't work out, I blamed myself for not being good enough. Many times I had sex with them to fix it. I begged them for attention and consideration. I now know that it had to be on their terms. That is what I accepted. Forget about me. Let me just take what I can get. I was so easy. The problem with all of that is that I was mad about the decision that I made. The whore could take it but I couldn't. I wanted so much more. I wanted what the men wanted for their daughters. When I didn't get that I cried. I am still crying over a man that lets me know, he doesn't want me.

What am I to him? I don't even know. We are friends but I am a secret. I am not good enough to be anything more. I try to smile when I talk to him .I try to play the game but I can't do it anymore. I can't cry anymore

And I hear' You don't have to cry"

I know God is telling me that I don't have to cry. He is wiping my tears. The prophesy ..he is going to give double .I believe it. Let me cry because I am filled with joy and I blessed by God. Don't let me cry because man has hurt me. I give man no power to make the tears fall from my face.

Oh God, take the tears of mine and me joy!

Oh God I don't wanna cry no more.

Let me take theses tears and use them in a praise for your glory.

I can't do it anymore.

On Trial

I put myself on trial for being the whore. If someone ask if I am innocent or guilty, I would say that I am guilty. That is the way I feel. I have so much guilt that I cry after I have been with a man. There is pain when I am with then because I know that they only want my body. After they have had me, I don't feel good enough and I feel unworthy to be loved. I feel like I have disappointed God. Many times, I have to defend myself and say I am not a whore.
Then ask myself, why do I feel like one .

Getting away from Satan wasn't and isn't easy. He always come back. I know I have a choice but that's the thing, it never felt like a choice. Every time he comes back ,I'm kicking and screaming
Some people will say that I knew exactly what I was doing. I could agree but not totally. I was misled. I was confused. I know, I knew it was wrong but what was I going to do. I was threatened. If I didn't do it, no one would love,
A few men have said that they did not see me as a whore, but they did. I could tell. My crime was giving myself to them and believing in them.

I now know what it feels like when men stop loving you and they are just having sex with you. I made them stop loving me because I could not bear to trust that they loved me. My comfort zone was sleeping with them . I believed that is how you show love.
When does it end? That's what I want to know. At least the women on the streets are real about who they are. They dress the part and they take the money. They tell you that it is not free.
Do I think that they pay the price for being out there in the streets. Yes, I do.
I thought that I was different from them. But I am not. They have their reasons just like me. They have accepted who they are. So should I accept being the whore?
Why does God want me to admit it now?

You know, I tell the story about my life to strangers and I am thinking. I don't know why. I just want to see the look in a person eyes. I want them to see me. There is a problem with that. When I tell me , they want the same things the other men had. They stop looking at me as a good woman and start treating me like a whore. I don't want to testify. I want to plead the fifth. I will not testify against myself.

142

I will not be a witness against myself.
The voice-But be a witness for God.

.

Rest In Him

What do you do when there is no peace? That was me. I couldn't get passed the whore no matter how fast I ran. The whore was my storm. In the Bible Jesus said to the storm "Peace be still"

And the storm was gone . I wondered, where was my peace. Being the whore isn't easy. You get thrown into it and you are on your own .There is no peace for a whore . One day, this stranger came up to me. She was a very nice lady. She told me that she doesn't always talk to strangers but she was led to talk to me. She didn't speak a Bible verse or anything like that. She just told me that God said to rest in him.

Then she left.

I was supposed to focus on him and sleep in his word. I was supposed to sleep in him.

Every time, I chose man, but when you get so tired and you don't have any other choice……

Holy spirit, "Just close your eyes"

And I rested in God.

Rest In Me-Poem

When you get tired and you don't have no choice.
You struggle just to survive .
But you have no power and you hear God's voice .
He's keeping you alive.
And you hear him say, rest in me. .
You fight it as best as you can.
But the more you try, the enemy fights to win .
And what can you do?
You hear God say rest in me.
You try but you can't go on.
You fight ,but you are not strong .
You do all that you can.
But you can't stand.
You can't help it, you close your eyes .
And you rest in him.

I Will Not Be Your Whore

I don't know what happened .Something happened and there
was a change in me. I could just hear myself saying no, no.
And I got louder. It was like I was opening a door with my
words.

I was telling Satan to get out .

You can't have my mind, my heart, my body or my soul!
Get out! Because you don't have any power. You got to go!
No, you will go. In the name of Jesus !

The whore did not have a voice but I did.

I will not be your whore anymore. I know it worked for you.
I gave you what you wanted, when you wanted it
And you didn't care about my tears.
You didn't care about loving me.
You wanted what you wanted.
I will not be you whore.
I will not give you what you want and let you feed off of my
shame.
You will not put me in the moment, I don't want to see your
face.
You can't pay me enough. I am not for sale.
There is nothing that you can say .
I am not your property. I am not your slave.
I can't say it enough.
I will not be your whore.
For you to a bruise, For you to use.
I will not be your whore.

And I meant it.

I Know Who I am

Then, God called me by my name and he said,

" I want to set the whore free because you prayed to be free.
The only way to do that is for you to see that she is not you
.she was never you . she was a lie. You didn't know who you
were and you didn't know the truth But now you know it
because I am telling you who you are. I am transforming you
into who you are."

145

When I think about what God said to me. I think about my ordination. See, my ordination certificate has my maiden name on it. Why? I didn't know why at first. I was told that it was a mistake. When I say my maiden name on it, I didn't think twice about it and I didn't ask for them to change it. Not until now that I really know why it had to be my maiden name. Because it doesn't belong to a man. I had to use my given name so no man could be attached to it. Then it had to be reprinted. It wasn't because of my last name. It was because I looked at it and I don't know, something was wrong. I didn't even know why I felt that way. Now I do. It was because the first print out had my name and just my name. It needed to say who I was .The second one needed to say evangelist.

I know it looks like a title. And that's what I didn't want was a title. To me a title means nothing. It's just something people call you. You can have a title and people will still treat you how they see you. If they do not believe in your title , you will not get the respect that your title holds. How they treat you is how they see you. So, I am forced to ask myself how do I see myself. I have worn the title of whore for most of my life and the funny thing is… my mom put that title on me and I wore it. It was choking the life out of me with my help. Nobody was really calling me the name whore . I was calling myself the whore. I was seeing myself like that and acting accordingly. But my spirit could not line up with my flesh. My spirit was still singing and still believing in God.

Everything about my spirit was God and everything about my flesh was a whore and in my mind I didn't know what to believe.

All I ever saw was the whore.

One More Time

I did it one last time. I slept with a man that I loved very deeply. It was supposed to be beautiful but I knew it wasn't going to be. You see we talked about having sex earlier and we both wanted to do it. I made up my mind to give him what he wanted. I remember asking him if he wanted this for his daughter. Would he want a man to just have sex with his daughter and give her nothing. I trusted the man to be honest but I believed he lied because he said that it was up to her. In the back of my mind, I knew he said it to make it okay for me to sleep with him. How could I fight that answer. He was telling me , it was my choice. He wasn't going to have any regrets if I slept with him. So, I had to prepare myself to sleep with him and not have any regrets. He came over in the middle of the night just for sex and I let him. I opened the door for him and I set the mood. When I was ready, we began and I did things to him that only a wife would do. I made sure not to ask for anything. I made sure to stay in control the whole time. He would remember me. As I did it, I told him how much I hated him and I showed him how much I loved him. I kept saying in my mind "I hate you" He

never knew. He never knew. When we were finished ,I fell asleep .He woke me up the next morning and he couldn't have sex with me again. My body wouldn't let me.

I like to think that God wouldn't let him.

God will only let the enemy do so much to you.

Satan tests us every day because he wants us to deny God but I realize that Satan cannot win. Even in our sin we should have a praise and the belief that god is who he says he is.

Many people will think that Satan won that night but he didn't.

Yes, I was wrong but I felt like I had to do it.

I had to love him with all of my heart , so that I could break the cycle and let go. I even prayed to God to forgive me because what I did was not out of lust. It was love and yes, I hated this man for only wanting this from me. He said it was too late to try with me . To me that meant it was too late to love me.

I can say that, that night I did not feel like the whore. I felt like a woman who was in love

But God says to love him. "A man's love will never be enough to sustain you".

I asked God why?

Because they can stop at any moment and at any time and give up on you.

God's love is unconditional and kind and because it is patient, God will not give up

Taking What I Could Get

Days went by, when I saw this man again. Inside, I was so happy to see him. I was willing to accept him for who he was. I said to myself, "I will take what I can get from him" I Even if it was friendship, I was going to take it.

Was I still the whore?

Even a whore knows her worth.

No I wasn't going to let him make me a whore ever again.

I just wanted to love him

"And when he hurts you, then what?"

That played in my mind while I waited for him to come by and pick up my dog to dog sit.

He didn't want me for nothing else. He just wanted to be friends.

Could I do it and not regret it. I knew if sex came up, I would sleep with him willingly and possibly opening a door for the whore

Oh God ,remove the desire from me and take away this feeling of pain!

You see I would take it if I had to.

You have to be desperate to be the whore. You have to want to hold on to love to give your body away.

I can't speak for everybody but that was me when I was deeply in love

I kept telling myself that if I took what he was willing to give me, it would work.; even if it hurt me to do it.

I didn't want to hear that it wasn't right and that I was better than that.

I kept seeing the vision of me and him happy. I kept telling myself we could be happy .

It was no longer about him loving or wanting a whore .

149

I wanted him to love me.

I was at work when I called him and asked him what time he would be over to get the dog. He was busy and I knew that. So I wasn't asking for a conversation .I wasn't upset.

But just because I wasn't upset and it wasn't a problem, it was a problem.

The conversation was so casual . He wasn't going to stay the night .He wasn't going to hold me. I was just a friend. I had to see that .

Wouldn't I make the best wife?

There is nothing like marrying your best friend

Even that was up for debate. When you have been a whore for so long, I wonder would I cheat on him.

I use to tell him that I needed attention. I thrived on it . so if he didn't give it to me, would I go find another man and lay up with that man then come back home to him.

A few days ago I might say maybe but I know that I don't have to find a man for attention and the price for that attention doesn't have to be sex.

I don't need that from him.

I can only hope and have faith and be there for him.

I thought about it. I can give everything and just take what he gives me but how soon before Satan has me again.

This man was making me weak and somehow tearing me down.

150

I was looking for him to build me up when God is the only one who can do that and who is willing to do it.

Breadcrumbs

If I thought about it the whore takes what she can get. She takes breadcrumbs. When you feel like you are not deserving of love you take whatever you can. The problem with that is, it is not a whole meal. Taking breadcrumbs will not fill you up.

The man that calls you once a week. The one who sees you when he needs something.

A man that doesn't love you fully gives you bread crumbs. I use to tell my boyfriend that he just gives me breadcrumbs and I don't want that. Back in the day a man use to take a woman out and feed her. Then he would want sex.

Don't I deserve a meal?

I want to know my worth. In the back of my mind, I think that a whore can take the breadcrumbs but I am more deserving. I have been starving all of this time .

I hear God saying but you didn't have to starve.

I know what it means. I was with the most wonderful person who I knew loved me but I couldn't love him. In my heart I did but my actions …

Do I regret my actions.

I can only say that I have accepted the things I have done and I take responsibility for what she did .

I Love You

I knew I wasn't the whore but I had to ask myself if the man that I loved knew it to.

He knew my whole story and he constantly chose to have sex with me. I wasn't even a girlfriend. I was classified as a friend .

I remember telling him that I gave him power and he looked at me

I said" You have the power to destroy me"

He said he didn't but I knew he did. It is always your actions that tell the truth.

We had sex one last time . After we had sex, he made a statement that it would probably not happen again. Maybe because he didn't want me.

Something was wrong with that. I mean I was hurt because he didn't want to have sex with me.

Satan was telling him what to say to hurt me.

You see, that's what men wanted and if they didn't want me something was wrong,

God-I want you.

Even when I didn't want to have sex, I still wanted the men to want me and I hated them for it .

That's why, when he said what he said, bothered me I thought, maybe he wasn't sure if I would do it. It would have to be my decision. But then I wondered, if he knew that God wouldn't let him.

I just keep hearing God.

"How long do you think I will let you hurt her and make her what you want her to be? She is not yours, she is mine. The man that will be with her will claim her. She will be his in every way. How long do you think I will let you play your games.? I claimed her before anyone else .She was never meant to be a whore. I can give her the world but the world is not what I have for her. I will give her all my love."

And then God spoke to me

"Remember when man does not love you, I do"

And I kept hearing God.

And I kept hearing God.

He kept saying he loved me.

"I love you more than man loves you .I love you without a condition. I love you. I love you "

Knowing that God loved me made me realize that I didn't have to have sex for man to love me.

They had nothing when I compared them to God.

I Have Looked In The Mirror

I have looked in the mirror and have seen myself completely.

See ,most of the times, when I looked at myself, I looked at myself in the darkness.

I couldn't be loved because I didn't love myself.

It never dawned on me to see myself in the light.

You might think that I am talking about turning on a switch. If only it was that simple. No ,I had to see myself in the word. And once I did that .....

Now, I can't see the whore because she doesn't exist. I see me and the Bible says your name shall be ministers.

You know, I realize that God looks at you and he sees who you are but he knows who you are going to be.

I looked at myself one way . I made up my mind who I was by another person's action and I chose not to love myself.

God chose to love me every day.

People will say that I was young. I will accept that, but now I am older and I do not see like a child. I see like a woman and I am beautifully made.

I have something to sing about when I should have nothing to sing about.

154

God made me whole that is the song I sing.

Split in two,

Broken into pieces,

Ripped apart,

My heart barely beating.

I thought it was over.

I thought it was the end.

No man could put me back together again.

Oh God, he came and he saw me.

He picked me up every piece.

And in his hands he made me whole.

Oh God he came and he saw me.

He picked me up every piece.

And in his hands he made me whole.

I was split into by that first touch. I was broken into pieces by what my family said. Now I am whole. I am whole by God's word.

God wanted me to look at myself and see what he sees. And once I did that the whore would be and is gone forever.

I made the whore another person because that's who I was when I had sex.

155

I learned all the tricks .Like they say "the tricks of the trade" and if it had of been one man… maybe then, I may not have seen myself the way I did but one became many an when people keep treating you that way ,what are you supposed to be.

Let me say this, because I looked at myself ,I forgave myself and those men. I thought it was crazy to forgive them and wondered how come I protected them. You see, I never told anyone their names.no one ever went to jail or had to stand in court. They did not have to be judged because of what I said . I even questioned myself while I wrote this.

Why am I protecting the guilty?

But just like I have changed, I have to believe that they have and believe that God will dealt with them.

You may think that this was about the whore but at the end of the day ,it was about who I became.

No matter what, my spirit still had a song for God and in all of this mess, my spirit could still see God.

Don't you know , in all of the darkness, there is still some glimpse of light.

There is God.

No matter, what I did or what was done to me, I still had a song for God. I confessed God. My spirit didn't die and out of my spirit emerged the evangelist.

The Demon named Anger

As I wrote this book, I didn't know how angry I was.

Who were you mad at

I was mad at myself. I can admit it now that I was molested. I still do not like the word or admitting it .I can say that but it's a word that needs to be said.

I wanted to give my testimony of how God delivered me from Anger.

Because I did not say anything as a child, I did not know that I was building up anger.

I was never mad at the men for touching me. Even when I was raped, I wasn't mad.

I was scared and ashamed.

I noticed that with my last boyfriend, I was getting angrier and angrier .Hate was in my heart. I did not know why. So, I had to write this book to find out why.

After all of the years to know that you stayed in a defensive mind set because you couldn't fight or know how to fight against a touch.

I lashed out at people because I felt ashamed and I couldn't tell nobody.

God used one particular man to make me deal with the molestation.

I believe that I had to remember.

As, I remembered, I found myself hating myself.

I constantly said that I never told and I was angry at myself for it. I didn't even know that I was mad .

I sat in church one Sunday morning feeling ..I don't know. I just didn't have a praise. Then all of a sudden, I could feel the Holy Ghost in the room and I began to shout. In a second I became ashamed and in my mind I was the six year old. I sat down on the floor trying not to be seen.

Did I praise God too hard?

I never liked feeling out of control.

I kept saying "I should have told someone, I should have told someone"

Then I heard God

"I brought you to this place to be delivered"

I said to myself, 'That is why I am here, to be delivered."

Satan did not want me to be delivered.

I heard someone say "Don't be embarrass ,come out and praise him "

But I couldn't move.

I began to run to wall and they tried to pull me out and then…

Woman after woman came to me. They prayed over me but anger said "You can't have her."

There was this woman who saw him and asked him his name but I couldn't say

Then I said anger.

Anger said, "Leave her."

But they wouldn't give up on me.

I was in and out. I responded to the Chief Apostle. She said my name.

Anger responded to another woman who had great power.

I remember being defiant on purpose.

They prayed again and again.

Then..

I don't know what happened but I broke free.

God broke the chains .

I was let out of the cage.

Anger was gone and there was peace.

I Don't Feel The Whore

Before that day, I could still feel the whore and my book wasn't finished but after that day ,I can no longer feel the whore.

A man asked me, not to long ago, if I needed a hotel room.

It was cold and I was at work. I couldn't go home

Normally, I would have said yes to his hotel idea and I would have prepared myself for sex. But this time I said no.

He said he would let me sleep on the couch and nothing would happen. Normally that would work. I would accept that(make myself believe it)

But I still said no

He made this statement "You will take a man's money but you won't have sex with him."

The answer was still no

Some people will look at me funny for telling my story. I can see them deciding not to talk to me .That is what kept me from seeing myself as anything but a whore. I realize that I can't keep this to myself. I had to tell this story for it was the only way to see myself as something beautiful. Writing about this part of my life set me free. I just didn't become free, I broke free.

The Letter

A friend of mine said I should see the man that touched me and tell him that he was wrong. At first, I dismissed the idea. Then, I looked for his name. I almost hoped that he was dead. I immediately prayed to God. I prayed that the man who touched me changed to who God wanted him to be.

After the prayer, I smiled because I know God had did it and that gave me such a peace.

Then I thought, why do I need to see him?

I don't want to seek him out. I thought, was I afraid to see him. Would he admit that he touched me? What would I say.? You know, I looked for his picture and I was afraid to see it because what if those emotions would came back.

I was worried because there was a chance that mentally I would become the age that he touched me and breakdown.

But I kept hearing God say "You are stronger than that"

Then I realized that it was not about seeing him. I could take my pen and write how he hurt me.

You hurt me..

You took something from and left me empty and you didn't care.

Your touch was a disease and it spread through my insides.

I should hate you but I couldn't when I was a child and now that I am older, I still can't.

I do pray that God dealt with you and if he hasn't yet, I pray he does and I hope you never hurt anyone else. I want you to know that you opened a door of pain and hurt and self-hatred in me. The moment you touched…I was wounded and the wounds would not heal. What you did to me was wrong

You don't have to say nothing or deny what you did because God knows what you did.

I forgive you .

I want you to know that despite what you did to me, God has healed me and he has closed the wound that you left. I want you to know that I don't have any scars.

This is not about what you did. I want you to see what God did.

Immediately, after I wrote that, I thought about Paul setting the prisoners free. Then this verse from Jeremiah came to me.

Jeremiah 30:8

In that day,' declares the Lord Almighty,

   'I will break the yoke off their necks

and will tear off their bonds;

   no longer will foreigners enslave them.

Some people look at the Bible as past events and because of that they cannot see God doing the same things in the present but see, I was taught that God does not change. His word is kept forever. He declared it and it is so .

Someone enslaved me by touching me. He was a foreigner. I knew him as a friend , but he became a stranger when he touched me the way he did . I was a prisoner by that touch but God declared that he would break the yoke (a wooden crosspiece that is fastened over the necks of two animals and attached to the plow or cart that they are to pull.) He said that he would tear off their bonds. "Break and tear". That means he would do it by force.

and that words no longer (used to say that something that was once true or possible is not now true or possible) it is a declaration in just the words.

No longer will I cry!

162

No longer will this hurt me

No Longer will I feel weak!

No longer will you be able to affect my life!

God said no longer will foreigners enslave them.

You do not have the capabilities to keep me as a slave

I started to continue with the letter but God said that I
finished it when I wrote

No longer will I cry!

No longer will this hurt me

No Longer will I feel weak!

No longer will you be able to affect my life!

God said no longer will foreigners enslave them.

You do not have the capabilities to keep me as a slave

And God said "Now you can say good-bye"

And you know, I was crying and I was smiling.

No, those emotions won't come back. I know that they
won't.. The child has grown up and I am not the whore but
an evangelist.

163

The Best of Me

Now I can see it.

See what?

The best of me. I never thought that I would get to this point in my life. I always felt ashamed for the sins I committed. I believe that God can use any situation for a purpose. Whatever I went through can be used for the purpose of God.

I once said that I never gave a man the best of me .I never tried but this time in my life, I would be ready to do that but I realize than I wasn't meant to give man the best of me because It is meant for God.

And if God gets the best of me , then that is all that matters.

That means I will love the best, have faith the best.

My light can only shine for God.

That's why the enemy had me in darkness, so I wouldn't shine .

I Quit

I have constantly said that I had a job to do and I made it sound like I didn't have a choice. I called it a job because that's how a whore would see it. It is work. I might have felt like it was love and it was fun but I want to say it again that over the course of time I changed and the job wasn't worth it anymore. It became a job. Because the feelings were not there. I had to make myself want to do it.

Why put yourself through that?

I know some people say that they like their work but if that is the case, why do whores want to leave the business?

And they may want to leave but still stay .They get so use to the day to day life and they tell their selves that they cannot get out. They forget what their dreams use to be.

You do not have to sleep with a million men to feel misused and to feel like nothing. One person , one man can make you feel unworthy.

How long will you work a job that is costing you to work there? You can't break even. It's not free to be a whore.

(that means someone treating you like one, abusing you, talking bad to you or cussing you out. Someone having sex with you and leaving to go to another woman's house, or someone not marrying you)

I quit my job. I quit seeing myself like a whore and I am happy about it. God said I was Ester. I am a queen!

The Ability To Love Again

After everything that I have been through and with all that I have learned and know, I am worried . Not about becoming the whore again but I am worried if I can love someone. I

165

guess you can say that I know too much .I have learned not to trust .so, how do I trust any man with my heart?

I keep thinking about how nice it would be to actually love someone and give them me but I wonder is it worth it.

I use to ask the question , who is going to love me?

Who is going to be there?

I do not ask that anymore because I know God is.

Now, I am just thinking, who can I love.

Will I be able to be with them.

Every part of physical intimacy , to me is defined as a whorish act.

I'd rather kiss you good night , than let you lay on top of me.

If something happens, I feel like I should be ashamed . I could enjoy the moment but I will have to deal with what happens next.

I am afraid to love fully and I do not know why I feel this way,

I'm looking for the moment that God says it is okay. That is not completely true. I want to feel that it okay to be loved and love someone back.

I have all these hopes and dreams to get it right because that is what I want but I wonder will I .

The Cover

The Bible says that God will use the foolish thing (the simplest thing)to compound the wise. God showed me this through the cover of my book. When I started writing the book (the book I did not want to write) , a picture came to my mind. I saw fishnet stockings. I knew that the fishnets represented the whore. And that was the beginning of my cover.

Once I saw the image of the fishnets, immediately I felt that I should have the cover created. I did not want to wait until I finished the book. So, I had the part that represented the whore The next part of the cover had to represent the evangelist. I thought that was going to be easy , but it wasn't.

I searched and searched for the right representation. Finally, I decided to do a preacher's robe It was a woman in a preachers robe holding a Bible. When the cover was finished, I thought it was okay, but it did not touch my soul. In spite of how I felt, I decided to go with it. I did not feel that I could redo it. In my mind, once a cover is done , it is done. There was no going back. But when I finished the book ,I realized that the cover did not work. In the cover you saw flesh but you did not see the spirit, the cover had to change It had to reflect who I was and who I am.

When I finished the cover , I saw me. I saw my spirit.

And I heard God say that the cover had to change . I couldn't change it because I felt like it couldn't change but he could change it and when he changes the cover everything changes.

A Prayer

I never want what happen to me to happen to anyone else. I don't want anyone to go through what I had to. In saying that, I know that it will happen again. Not to me but to someone else.

God,

Let no weapon be formed that can destroy them. Whatever is taken from them, give it back to them. Take that which is old and make it new.

God, do not let them hold on to any pain or hurt and if they are crying God

Wipe their tears.

Let no wicked, evil touch be like a disease to their body. God heal them from every touch that was not meant for good,

God , send your angels down to comfort them and wrap your arms around them.

Don't let them stay there , in the moment where the hurt began but let them rise up like an eagle and fly in the wind.

Give them strength and courage to speak out.

Don't let the touches of man silence them

Give them a voice when the enemy takes it away.

God, let them know that they are beautiful and no man has the power to change or recreate what you have already made.

Let them see that you created them and they were good.

Fill them up God, when they fill empty.

Let them not be tormented or kept in a prison from a touch

God set them free. And let them know that once they are free, they will always be free.

Amen.

Psalms 23

It's funny how God deals with me and shows me things. The other day, I kept thinking about Psalms 23 and then a friend of mine mention the color purple. She said that was her favorite color.

When she said purple, I immediately thought of love and Psalms 23.

23 The LORD is my shepherd; I shall not want.

² He maketh me to lie down in green pastures: he leadeth me beside the still waters.

³ He restoreth my soul: he leadeth me in the paths of righteousness for his name's sake.

⁴ Yea, though I walk through the valley of the shadow of death, I will fear no evil: for thou art with me(remember the man on the phone. He said, why should he be afraid when God is there) ; thy rod and thy staff they comfort me.

(God never changes. He doesn't love one more than the other. He comforted me in those moments when there was no one.)

[5] Thou preparest a table before me in the presence of mine enemies☺God shows he loves me when he takes the time to prepare a blessing for me. He doesn't do it in secret. He does it for the world to see) thou anointest my head with oil; 9I remember combing my mother's hair and how special that was to her. I did it because I love her. For God to anoint you that means he sees something in you . he loves you)my cup runneth over.

[6] Surely goodness and mercy shall follow me all the days of my life: and I will dwell in the house of the LORD forever.

I heard God say that he loves me in Psalms 23.

Many people see how much David loved God and I see that to, but in Psalms, David talks about all the things that God did for him

David tells you about God's kindness.

I see the love of God is Psalms.

Over and over again I hear

" I love you, I love you"

He loves me and his love does not cost me anything.

The love of a man cost me my life. Over and over, in some way, I died.

And every time God gave me life. He wouldn't just let me die.

I never had to ask for anything when it came to God.

I had peace and comfort.

Everything that he does speaks love.

This was never about the whore but who I am today.

I find myself blessed. To go through life and still come out alive. Most people say that they should have been dead. I agree. The enemy tried it but I get a chance to liv one more day to tell my story.

Up Coming Books:

Who Wants A Dead Baby?

In The Beginning Was The Word

I Know Who I Am

I have been writing for over forty years and I thank God for the ability .

This book is my testimony.

I hope it blesses you and if nothing else, let's you know that you can be free .

And know that an addiction cannot define you.

Made in the USA
Monee, IL
31 May 2022